D1570870

LEVERAGED BUYOUTS

LEVERAGED BUYOUTS

edited by Stephen C. Diamond

DOW JONES-IRWIN Homewood, Illinois 60430

This publication is designed to provide accurate and
authoritative information in regard to the subject matter
covered. It is sold with the understanding that the
publisher is not engaged in rendering legal, accounting, or
other professional service. If legal advice or other expert
assistance is required, the services of a competent
professional person should be sought.

*From a Declaration of Principles jointly adopted by a Committee
of the American Bar Association and a Committee of Publishers.*

ISBN 0-87094-579-3

Library of Congress Catalog Card No. 84–73255

Printed in the United States of America

67890K210987

*To the entrepreneur,
without whom leveraged buyouts
would not exist.*

Preface

No publication on leveraged buyouts can be timeless. There are variations in technique from deal to deal, and players introduce nuances with alacrity. Although certain basic underlying issues remain constant, approaches and solutions may vary with time. This is particularly true, for example, of tax-related issues.

It is the purpose of this book to highlight those issues which are essential to permit the reader to develop a meaningful frame of reference regarding leveraged buyouts. The end result should not be confused with a "how to" textbook—which this publication does not profess to be.

Biographies

Gary B. Anderson is chairman of Pelron Corporation. In the past 10 years, he has acquired over 12 firms ranging from $500,000 to $55 million in sales. Industries represented have varied from service to heavy manufacturing. Mr. Anderson has been both a borrower and a lender. He received an M.B.A. in finance from Northwestern and a B.A. in finance from Northern Illinois University.

H. Bruce Bernstein is a senior partner in the law firm of Sidley & Austin and a member of the National Bankruptcy Conference. He is a former chairman of both the Chicago Bar Association Commercial Law Committee and the Illinois State Bar Association on Commercial, Banking, and Bankruptcy law. Mr. Bernstein received his A.B. from Cornell University and his J.D. degree from Harvard Law School. He has written several articles on corporate reorganization and secured lending topics and has lectured widely on Uniform Commercial Code, Bankruptcy Code, and related subjects.

John A. Canning, Jr. is senior vice president of the First National Bank of Chicago. He is a director of a number of companies and a member of both the Chicago and Illinois Bar Associations. Mr. Canning received his A.B. from Denison University and his J.D. from Duke University.

Leonard S. Caronia is vice president and head of the Corporate Finance Division of the First National Bank of Chicago. His division specializes in the private placement of taxable and tax-exempt financing and in structuring leveraged buyout transactions. Mr. Caronia has given a number of presentations to industry groups, accounting organization, and commercial banks on the availability and structuring of long-term financing. He holds B.S. and M.B.A. degrees from the University of Illinois.

Stephen C. Diamond is senior vice president of the First National Bank of Chicago and is the senior credit officer of its newly formed corporate banking department. He was formerly chairman of First Chicago Credit Corporation, which is responsible for First Chicago Corporation's asset-based lending and vendor finance activities. Previous to that he was president of Chase Commercial Corporation. Mr. Diamond is immediate past chairman of the National Commercial Finance Association. Mr. Diamond attended Stanford University and the University of Southern California Law School, where he was an associate editor of the Law Review. He is a member of both the California and Illinois Bar Associations.

Mark H. Friedman is managing director of Mergers and Acquisitions for American Can Company. He has been at American Can since 1976 and has been a lead participant in numerous divestitures and acquisitions, including the sale of Dixie-Northern to James River in 1982 and the sale of M & T Chemicals to Elf-Acquitane in 1977. Mr. Friedman has been active professionally in mergers and acquisitions for over 15 years as an investment banker, financial intermediary, and corporate executive. He received his A.B. from Cornell University and his M.B.A. from Columbia University.

Joseph A. Kitzes is a CPA and partner with Seidman & Seidman and is Midwest regional technical director of Accounting and Auditing. He earned his B.B.A. degree from the City College of New York. He is an active member of the AICPA and presently serves as chairman of the Auditing Procedures Committee.

Donald H. Lamb is a tax manager with Seidman & Seidman. He earned his B.S.B.A. and M.B.A. degrees from Bowling Green State University and his M.S.T. degree from De Paul University. He is a member of the Illinois Society of CPAs as well as the AICPA.

James A. Long is senior vice president, Mergers & Acquisitions, with American Can Company. He joined American Can in 1975 as manager, Asset Management after serving with the Sperry and Hutchinson Company in various financial management positions. Mr. Long received a B.A. degree from Dartmouth College in 1964 and an M.B.A. degree in finance in 1966 from Columbia University Graduate School of Business.

Joseph S. Schuchert is managing partner of Kelso & Company, an investment banking firm specializing in divestitures and leveraged buyouts utilizing employee stock ownership plan (ESOP) financing techniques. He is also the managing partner of Kelso Partners, the general partner of Kelso Investment Associates II which makes equity investments in ESOP leveraged buyouts. Mr. Schuchert has participated in the design and installation of a wide variety of ESOP programs throughout the United States, both for major U.S. corporations and for small, closely held businesses, since joining Louis O. Kelso in 1970. (Mr. Kelso's activities as an economist, author, and lawyer led to the development of the ESOP.) Mr. Schuchert is a graduate of Carnegie Mellon University (B.S., electrical engineering) and the University of Pittsburgh Law School.

Contents

Part I

Leveraged Buyouts

An Introduction

Chapter 1

Introduction and Overview

Leveraged buyouts have recently received high visibility in the press, so one may get the impression that they are a relatively new phenomenon. They are not! We will explain the history of this type of financing, but first let's establish some definitions that will be used throughout this book.

DEFINITIONS

A leveraged buyout (LBO) is any acquisition of a company which leaves the acquired operating entity with a greater than traditional debt-to-worth ratio. The structure of the credit will always fall into one of the following quadrants:

		Type of financing	
		Secured	Unsecured
Type of transaction	Asset acquisition		
	Stock acquisition		

Type of Financing

Secured financing occurs when the assets of the acquired operation are used to collateralize the debt. The difference between the secured debt and the purchase price is normally covered by a combination of equity contribution of the investing group and notes taken back by the seller.

Unsecured financing normally involves some combination of venture capital, "mezzanine debt" (subordinated debt, generally with an equity kicker, and senior debt (generally owing to banks), aggregating to the total purchase price.

Type of Transaction

Asset acquisitions involve the formation of a new corporation (or utilization of an existing corporation), which acquires the assets of the target company. Asset acquisitions are generally easier to document, but they often raise significant tax issues which can affect the purchase price. If the acquired operation is a corporate division rather than a separate corporation, an asset acquisition is the only available type of transaction.

Stock acquisitions take many forms: They can include stock redemptions, tender offers, pure stock acquisitions, and reverse mergers. They generally involve the most complex structuring and the greatest number of legal issues. They are most commonly used if the target company is publicly held or if an asset acquisition will result in significant tax issues.

Throughout this book there will be reference to the following terms:

Target company is the company being acquired.

Selling company is the corporate owner of the target company before the LBO.

Holding company is the corporate vehicle used to make the acquisition. It may be an existing corporation or a new corporation formed for the purpose of acquiring the target company.

HISTORY

Secured leveraged buyouts have been with us for some time. During the heavy conglomerating era of the 1960s, a number of entrepreneurs formed miniconglomerates through the use of leveraged buyouts. The lender was normally a commercial finance company; commercial banks were not yet in this business. The acquired company was normally a smaller company—generally with less than $20 million of sales volume. The underlying collateral for the loan was the accounts receivable, inventories, and fixed assets of the acquired company.

In many cases the investor had no equity risk; in some, he was not even asked to personally guarantee the loan. For that reason, this type of financing was often called "bootstrap" financing—the entrepreneur could lift himself by his own bootstraps into a position of wealth and success. The lender normally insisted on adequate security, measured in terms of distressed liquidation values, and the thrust of the lender's analysis was directed toward collateral coverage rather than toward cash flow. Because each transaction was relatively small, the flow of deals went virtually unnoticed except by those who were actively engaged in the business.

Fairly late in the 1960s a second type of leveraged buyout began to emerge. This type involved situations where a lender would take an equity kicker and subordinate its debt, rather than taking collateral. The combination of equity and subordinated debt would entice another group of unsecured lenders to lay on a level of senior debt, since the target company's cash flow could clearly service such senior debt. The subordinated debt holders, initially limited to a small group of aggressive insurance companies, were willing to take a significant downside risk for an even more significant upside gain. Because no one was secured in the transaction, however, the analytical emphasis by all financing sources was on cash flow rather than on collateral.

Both secured and unsecured lenders had certain common criteria. Since in both cases an additional layer of debt was being imposed on the target company, with additional debt-servicing requirements, a company that was incurring heavy losses would not normally be a target for a leveraged buyout unless the loss was clearly a short-term phenomenon that could be quickly reversed. Second, the lenders in both cases normally wanted to have continuity of management, and most leveraged buyouts involved the management group's continued involvement. To assure this, the management group would often be given some part of the equity. In many cases, in fact, the driver behind the leveraged buyout was the management group itself, although in a number of cases a third-party entrepreneur would promote the acquisition.

An offshoot of this was the leveraged buyout partially funded through an employee stock ownership program. Louis Kelso, who developed the ESOP, initiated this segment of the market. He first used it in 1956 to acquire a small newspaper chain for its managers and employees. Mr. Kelso's firm, Kelso & Company, is the most visible firm engaged in full-scale ESOP investment banking, although a few other San Francisco–based firms, generally staffed with principals who at one time worked with Kelso, function as ESOP specialists and legal consultants. Joseph Schuchert, who is president of CEO of Kelso & Company, contributed Chapter 8 to this book. The reader should note, in reading that chapter, that Mr. Kelso originally designed the ESOP because of his belief that a broader ownership of capital is critical to the long-term economic prosperity and political stability of this country.

While the seeds of the leveraged buyout boom were planted in the 1960s or before, the climate for growth was fostered during the latter half of the 1970s. Although there has long been a universe of closely held companies involving principals seeking to sell their companies in order to liquify their holdings, these tend to be smaller companies. The first highly visible large leveraged buyout involved the acquisition of the Houdaille Machinery Company and was orchestrated by Kohlberg, Kravis, Roberts & Co. This landmark acquisition both established a leadership role for KKR in structuring unsecured leveraged buyouts and extended the application of leveraged buyouts to a size of transaction that had not been previously contemplated. It basically opened the eyes of both corporate America and Wall Street to a new method of divestiture from the seller's standpoint and significantly increased the universe of potential buyers.

The economy also played a big part. The inflationary environment of the 1970s encouraged secured financings, since the fixed assets that often served as collateral for a portion of the loan would actually appreciate with time rather than depreciate. Secured lenders therefore had a greater margin for error, since the underlying collateral was increasing in value at the same time the loan was being repaid, resulting in a significant decrease of risk. Buyers also liked inflation. The borrowed dollars would be repaid at future dates at a value discounted by the impact of inflation. For a time, you will recall, the prime rate was less than the underlying inflation rate, with the result that buyers were getting essentially free financing.

In addition, the economy encouraged divestitures. With the severe economic cyclicality we had in the 1970s and early 1980s, sellers wanted to unload companies that could not earn a targeted internal rate of return, and the "hurdle rate," which was stated as a minimally acceptable return on investment (ROI), was increased as a function of inflation. The more inflationary the environment, therefore, the more operations a company would seek to divest. Furthermore, the more uncertain the economic environment, the greater the probability of inadequate operating results. The highly unpredictable economy of the late 1970s and early 1980s significantly increased the number of divestiture candidates.

Finally, adding additional weight to the recent wave of corporate divestitures has been an increased focus in corporate boardrooms on strategy. Boards of directors began to recognize that each corporation had an identifiable corporate culture and could conduct certain activities well and other activities less well. Not only was making money in a number of different and diverse businesses getting increasingly difficult; it began to be recognized that most management teams could not run and manage significantly different businesses as well as they could groupings of synergistic businesses. The theory that a bright corporate generalist could manage anything has lost, during the past several years, its once-held, almost universal acceptance. There thus evolved a strategic focus on divestiture which drove companies to divest businesses that no longer met the long-term strategic requirements of the corporate parent.

Divestiture targets therefore generally fell into one of the following categories:

- Companies, generating an inadequate return on investment to the seller, which might, if more highly leveraged, return an adequate return to the buyer. While absolute dollar profitability would decrease due to the imposition of an additional interest load, ROI would escalate because of the reduced equity base.
- Companies showing an inadequate return to the seller which, freed from allocated corporate overhead and mandatory corporate processes, could earn a satisfactory return in a more entrepreneurial environment.

  Companies earning an adequate return on equity which did not fit into the long-term strategic plans of the selling corporation.

As many potential sellers turned to their investment bankers for structuring advice, the Wall Street community began to recognize that, since increased leverage could increase return on investment to the buying group, there might be a higher purchase price available to the seller through a leveraged buyout than through a negotiated sale to another major corporation; at the same time, the price of admission for a buyer could be paid with little equity and considerable debt. A number of investment bankers capitalized on this phenomenon by purchasing for their own account. This broadened the base of people seeking leveraged buyouts and tended to further drive the acquisition price up.

As the number of deals began to expand, more lenders decided to get into the game. Particularly during 1982 and 1983, when commercial loans flattened because of a soft economy and conventional lending spreads shrank due to high liquidity in the banking system, lenders saw a heavy investment in leveraged buyouts as a means of significantly building their loan portfolios while driving up return on assets. Their interest continued, even with the economic recovery and increased loan demand, because of the attractive spreads and front-end fees LBO financing generated. And so, during the past few years, we have seen an increasing number of deals available, an increasing number of buyers seeking to make an acquisition, and an increasing number of financiers seeking to finance a transaction.

Unfortunately, as was the case with real estate investment trusts and energy loans, the curve cannot ascend indefinitely. The strategic divestiture programs of most sophisticated corporations have been going on for a number of years, and the pace of strategic divestitures promises to slow down in the future. The economy has improved and the rate of inflation has decreased, both portending a decline in the number of financial divestitures. The short-term prognosis, then, is for a decrease in the amount of good deals available but a continued increase in the amount of potential buyers and lenders who are still reading yesterday's newspapers. The bottom line is a disequilibrium between supply and demand, which has been driving prices up to excessive levels and significantly increasing the risk:reward ratios for buyer and lender alike, although significantly benefiting the sellers. This is particularly evident in management-generated leveraged buyouts, where the seller has no motivation to sell and the inducement to the seller must be a purchase price in excess of the target company's intrinsic value.

The market today has cooled off slightly from the frenzied part of early 1984, and presents some pockets of opportunities. There are good deals available that can benefit all parties. The problem is that they are hard to find. A large percentage of deals are priced too high in relation to the potential payback for the risks they offer. Smart investors are picking and choosing their opportunities very carefully. Less intelligent buyers are driven by the emotional desire to own a business rather than by the financial dynamics of the operation itself.

The probable scenario, then, is that there will be a fallout from leveraged buyouts. Some financial institutions which have lent too aggressively will be hurt. Some private investors who were overly optimistic in buying "junk" bonds issued in connection with failed LBOs will complain. Some buyers who have paid too high a price will regret their decision. A brief anti-LBO culture will develop, proclaiming that leveraged buyouts are inherently bad. This is all to be expected, and similar reactions occur whenever a financial fad is overused. The sound businessman, however, will not fall victim to these generalities and will pick and choose his opportunity carefully.

While generically leveraged buyouts are neither a sure way of accumulating wealth nor a sure path to failure, intelligent choice supported by sound analysis can now, and will in the future, be a means of achieving capital accumulation. It is becoming, however, an increasingly difficult path to follow.

OVERVIEW OF SUBSEQUENT CHAPTERS

The chapters of this book are designed to give you a step-by-step perspective of how to proceed with a leveraged buyout. The book is designed not for the academician but for the readers of *Venture* and *Inc.* who want to get a little better understanding of the issues involved. It is written with the thought that its audience will have a broad range of backgrounds. It is also written with the intention of permitting would-be entrepreneurs to look hard at themselves and determine whether they are willing to make the commitment of time and energy and to take the degree of risk that is critical to entrepreneurial success. The payoff can be great—but the success rate is low.

To give the book an appropriate focus, the contributors are all people who make their living structuring LBOs. We will touch on aspects that have applicability to all sizes of transactions, although our primary focus will be on the deal under $50,000,000. We will not, however, address a very visible part of today's LBO activity—the hostile tender offer. The editor believes that the hostile tender offer is a misuse of a basically sound business concept.

Our starting point is some counsel and advice on how to find the deal. This is unquestionably the most difficult chore of a potential acquirer. The more one relies on a network of financial intermediaries to locate a target company, the greater the likelihood the deal will be shopped—particularly if the buyer is not already an established player. Developing a network of referral sources is the gate that must be entered before one can even play on the course. Once one spots a situation that appears attractive, a meaningful business plan has to be prepared. The critical issues revolve around cash flow and recognition of vulnerabilities. The business plan should address these issues on a monthly basis for the first year and on a slightly more macro basis as time progresses. The plan should not be a thick marketing piece designed to sell the financier; it should be a tight document addressing all aspects of the business, designed primarily to check whether all the areas of risk have been identified and attacked, and only secondarily addressed to the financing sources. Gary B. Anderson, contributing author of Chapter 2, has spent 10 years of his life in doing deals, making payrolls, and adjusting to environmental changes; he speaks from sound, practical experience.

We will then look at the LBO from the seller's perspective. Mark Friedman and James Long have negotiated a number of LBOs, pursuant to a defined divestiture program, for their employer. Their experiences shed a different light on some of the issues the buyer must face.

Once the deal has been spotted and a business plan prepared, financing becomes critical. Whether to seek secured or unsecured financing will be addressed in this section. We will open with a discussion of the secured LBO, the type of structure most generally used for smaller transactions. Then Leonard Caronia—who has successfully structured dozens of unsecured leveraged buyouts, determining the appropriate quantity of senior debt, mezzanine debt, and equity required—will speak to unsecured structuring. Finally, John Canning, who heads one of the country's premier venture capital firms, will talk to the role of the venture capitalist.

A specialized form of leveraged buyout involves the employee stock ownership plan. Joseph Schuchert is president and CEO of Kelso & Company, ESOP investment bankers. Mr. Schuchert has contributed chapter 8, The Art of the ESOP Leveraged Buyout.

There is significant intertwining of legal, tax, and accounting aspects of structuring a leveraged buyout, from the perspective of the buyer, the seller, and the financing source. H. Bruce Bernstein, a partner of Sidley & Austin, one of the nation's premier law firms, is among the leading attorneys in the country representing lenders financing leveraged buyouts. Seidman & Seidman, a major national accounting firm, has built its practice around dealing with entrepreneurs; two members of the firm, Joseph Kitzes and Donald Lamb, are uniquely qualified to speak to the accounting tax issues involved with these transactions.

We think you'll find the various perspectives of these highly qualified professionals more enlightening than could be the work of any single author.

Chapter 2

Defining the Game Board

Gary B. Anderson

IDENTIFYING THE PLAYERS AND FINDING THE DEAL

During the past several years, the leveraged buyout has emerged as an attractive vehicle for both individuals and corporations—for the former, to increase wealth; for the latter, to expand product lines. Like any creative business transaction where financing and business savvy are paramount, the LBO comes with its share of problems. But if you're equipped with a solid understanding of just how the game is played and if you can meet its unique challenges, the rewards of the LBO can be tremendous.

By definition, an LBO involves leveraging (borrowing) from a financing source to acquire the target company. The proceeds are used to pay the seller. Internal cash flow and/or asset redeployment are used to retire the debt. The buyers and sellers of target companies can be varied in motives and diverse in approaches. If you are a buyer, your first priority is to define what you are looking for: to determine the range of quality and the size of a firm you would consider purchasing. Having done that, you must find a deal that meets your target screen, locate the seller, determine what the seller is really attempting to accomplish (is it maximum price or some more intangible objective?), and then convince him you can deliver. We will discuss these aspects in this chapter.

Defining an Acceptable Range of Quality

It's foolish for you to spend your time looking at deals that are of a size or business profile that you wouldn't consummate if you could. You will save yourself significant lost motion by predefining a "range of quality" of prospective target companies. Ideally we all would like to buy a growing, profitable company at a bargain price. And we'd probably like to have proprietary products, simple manufacturing and distribution processes, and no labor problems. Unfortunately such opportunities are rare. That does not mean, however, that you must be indiscriminate in seeking a deal.

Most target companies are available for a reason. The company may have lost money, it may be capital intensive, or the market may be turning against it. Some available firms are burdened with significant problems. Of course, the seller isn't going to volunteer the real reasons it seeks to divest. The buyer is expected to uncover the issues, examine them, and be prepared to address them. If you're equipped to cope with the problems, go for the deal; if not, stop before you elect to pursue it.

The truth is, an overly emotional buyer may end up taking undesirable shortcuts in order to get the deal closed. Feeling that intense investigation will offend the seller and anxious to make the deal, he either may not probe adequately or may compromise his standards. This is especially true if it's the acquirer's first leveraged buyout. As one transacts more LBOs, the acceptable range of standards can be raised because an entrepreneur may not want to risk the capital base already generated. But the first deal must be closed before one can look at the second.

This is all understandable. However, you will normally regret the decision if you deviate from predetermined standards set before negotiations begin, without the interplay of emotion. Sit down, rank your priorities, and define minimally acceptable standards for all aspects of the business you want to own. If your expertise is in manufacturing, consider whether you would be willing to acquire a distributor. If your strength is in finance, consider whether you should look at a company whose problem is in generating sales. Define the universe of companies that is acceptable to you. If the target falls outside this universe, terminate the talks. It takes self-discipline to do so, and it may be difficult—especially if it is your first LBO. But it's an important rule to follow in the leveraged buyout game, and you'll be wise to stick to it firmly.

Defining the Targeted Size Range

When you address the size of the potential buyout, you'll need to keep in mind some basic realities. The larger the deal is, the greater attention you will get from both the lender and the seller. However, particularly if you've never done a leveraged buyout before, it will undoubtedly be more difficult to get financing for a midsized or larger ($5 million plus) buyout than for a smaller one. So spend some time honestly evaluating what you have to offer as a buyer before approaching the seller. This is no time for self-deception.

The LBO Players: Who Are the Sellers?

There are primarily three groups of potential sellers of an LBO target: (1) privately held firms that are for sale, for any number of reasons; (2) divisions or subsidiaries of larger corporations that are to be spun off; and (3) publicly held firms which are positioned in the marketplace for a possible takeover. Each group comes with a separate set of issues that the buyer must examine.

Privately Held Firms. Information pertaining to privately held firms that are for sale is very difficult to uncover. This is true largely because secrecy is often meaningful to a seller. Many owners have a desire to cash out their holdings but don't want to publicize it for fear that public knowledge will affect their customer relationships and their employee morale. In some cases the fear is justified, but in most cases the owners are overly concerned. After all, if someone really wants to sell, how can he expect to do so unless he talks to potential buyers? I've observed over many years that the perceived risks of employee or customer abandonment normally do not occur once an owner decides to sell. In fact, I've personally never seen it happen on a significant scale, although I have seen the occasional loss of a limited number of key employees. Nevertheless, these perceptions are real to the seller, and they do make it tough to obtain leads on private firms that are up for sale. (Later in this chapter, this group as a source of potential buyouts is discussed further.)

Divestitures. Divestitures of subsidiaries or divisions of corporations are a prime source of potential buyouts; unfortunately they are the most difficult for an individual purchaser to close. The positive aspect about these transactions is that you are usually dealing with sellers who are unemotional about the price and the terms of the offer. Thus you can enter and close the deal relatively quickly. The problem, however, is the competition relating to the purchase. The seller often uses a buyer's bid as a lever to elicit a higher bid. If the transaction is a tender offer, arbitrageurs may disrupt the pricing or even prevent the successful tender. Despite this difficulty, divestitures are probably the most fruitful place to find potential leveraged buyouts.

Publicly Held Firms. Publicly owned firms are in a unique category. With these firms, you have the benefit of obtaining data regarding financial evaluations of the potential buyout. But there are some real problems you must overcome. One is the unwieldy number of decision makers regarding the sale of the firm: the Securities and Exchange Commission (SEC), the stockholders, the board of directors, and frequently the management. Another problem is getting a firm hand on the collateral value of the assets. Although you have access to public information, you cannot get the additional information required to secure financing, in most cases, until management allows you to do so. This problem can be ultimately resolved, but it takes a good game plan to do so.

More about the Players: Who Are the Buyers and What Are Their Goals

We've discussed the sellers—your marketplace. Now, what about the buyers—your competition?

Buyers fall into one of three categories: (1) individuals, (2) large corporations, and (3) smaller corporations, normally closely held.

Individual Buyers. This group of buyers is a special breed; it probably comprises the core of potential buyers. Its membership comes from all walks of life. The participants seek acquisitions for a variety of reasons, and their objectives are as diverse as their personalities. Logically one might conclude the primary motivator is capital accumulation. It is for some, but for an equal number—in fact the majority of individuals that I've come across—the prime motivator is ego.

These people want to control an operation that is theirs, control their own destiny, set their own policies, and escape from a corporate bureaucracy. Unfortunately, although an individual motivated by capital accumulation tends to be logical, an individual driven by ego may become overly emotional. This can lead to inadequate analysis of the real value of the target company. Sometimes this class of buyers is concerned more with size than with profits and asset management. These would-be entrepreneurs may focus on perceptions of success rather than on achieving real financial success.

It takes a unique combination of talents to identify, negotiate, and manage a buyout. My experience is that only a few individuals demonstrate true managerial ability along with their entrepreneurial drive. This lack of management expertise will be reflected shortly after the euphoria of closing the deal passes. Most potential acquirers think that 80 percent of the work is getting the deal. In reality, that is only a starting point—the bulk of the work must be done after the deal is booked.

One other aspect of the individual buyer's personality must be weighed. LBO buyers are risk takers by definition. The more successful ones manage risk, while others cloud their judgment with excessive optimism. The second category of buyer does not necessarily understand the risks inherent in a given prospective buyout. Optimism coupled with sound analysis can overcome many difficulties; but optimism unaccompanied by sufficient forethought can lead to being blindsided when a real problem does appear.

Larger Corporations. The larger corporations acting as buyers in a buyout have a different motive. They want to increase their earnings per share. Ego may drive a few to seek volume increases for volume's sake, but this is the exception. Most larger corporations are driven primarily by short-term earnings and secondarily by long-term earnings. This is, after all, what keeps professional management in place. Done properly, the buyout enables the corporate buyer to add incremental earnings per share. Usually the interest of a larger corporation focuses on the larger deals—in excess of $50 million and going to hundreds of millions of dollars. The constraint it has is the resulting balance sheet. If the company is a normal user of the credit markets, covenants will limit its maximum leverage. Thus larger corporations, while often acquirers, are not normally doing true leveraged buyouts. However, they may be competing with an LBO group for an acquisition.

Smaller Corporations. Smaller corporations or privately owned midsized companies are a hybrid of the classic entrepreneurial one-time LBO buyer and the larger corporate, publicly held entity. They tend to be less emotional than (but often as ego oriented as) the first-time acquirer, with more focus on cash flow and less focus on earnings per share than the large, publicly held company. When compared to the individual buyer, they are often more professional, and often they have deeper pockets than an individual investor. They also have a proven track record that enhances their credibility with potential sellers.

The Hunt Is On: Finding the Deal

With this as background, let's move on to the first hurdle: Just where do you find leveraged buyouts? I'm going to address that question by first telling you where you probably will *not* find them. Ironically, this false path is the one many novitiates take when they are shopping.

Most inexperienced people who are looking for LBO prospects will talk to their accountants, their lawyers, and possibly the trust department of their local bank. My experiences have demonstrated that these are not good sources for leads—especially if this is your first time out on the block. For one thing, you're competing against many seasoned veterans, and they'll always get first bite at any deals—because they have the credibility. Your accounting and law firms, if they know of a division or company that's up for sale, have a responsibility to their clients to make sure the deal will go through without unnecessary snags. They may pay you lip service, but they'll probably give the lead to someone they can absolutely count on to get the deal closed.

How do you get over this hurdle? The truth is, you normally don't until you've made a few leveraged buyouts. How, then, do you get into the starting gate? It isn't a bad idea for a newcomer to enter the buying party with a partner. That partner can appear to carry much of the weight, so that when you walk into a law firm or accounting firm, you have instant credibility. Your story, for example, may be that there are three partners involved, two of whom are wealthy individuals and one of whom is you. The trade-off is obvious. Your wealthy partners are leveraging their capital and letting you do the grunt work. All parties benefit initially by this type of team. Your alternative—of attempting to do it all yourself the first time out—is, of course, a possibility. So is buying a $1 lottery ticket and winning $1 million.

You're limited in another way if you rely on accountants, lawyers, or bankers for leads. They are rarely marketing oriented, and that means they are not tuned to acting on business opportunities. By the nature of their professions, they are not trained to sniff out leads and pass them along. More often, they might come up with an idea—offhandedly—of possibly recommending to a person that he might want to consider selling or that they know of someone who might be interested in buying. This lack of marketing sensitivity, the fact that a lot of other people are vying for their time, and the relatively few leads that come their way make accountants, lawyers, and bankers less than ideal sources for leads. While there are exceptions to this rule, unless you're fortunate to be close to a deal-making professional, time spent soliciting these lead sources will generally be relatively nonproductive.

Where, then, do you go? Over the years I've discovered three good sources of finding leveraged buyouts. They are a bit unique, but they work; I highly recommend using them if you want to start building a base.

Start with Insurance Agents. The most probable source is an insurance agent. I've obtained more credible leads from this source than from any other. By the very nature of their business the more successful agents are well connected—often to top people they've dealt with for years and years. They're persistent. They're innovative. They've got the confidence of their clientele. Best of all, they're aggressive. You can suggest a finder's fee to them, and they'll seek it like they seek their insurance commissions. They're more than willing to stick their necks out and say to someone, "Would you like to sell your firm? I have a friend who might be interested in buying."

Cultivate ongoing contacts with as many well-established insurance people as you can. It's better to deal with people who have been in the business for many years. Their contacts are numerous, and they've developed trust with their clients. They have access to financial information, and they understand the meaning of this information. In the last 10 years, I've received at least 50 or 60 leads from three good agents. That certainly attests to how good a source insurance people can be—if you find the right ones.

As a side benefit, they can also be sources for capital in case you need some working capital or some equity infusion. Being sales oriented, the last thing they want to do is get involved with the operations. But they may be quite interested in putting up some money.

Stockbrokers and individual portofolio managers may fit into this category also. The appropriate profile includes (1) access to the right contacts and (2) the willingness to pursue these contacts in the interest of earning income.

A Divisional Sell-Off Can Signal Others. The second-best category of gathering leads is reading about larger companies that have announced a sell-off of one of their divisions. Of course, such an announcement doesn't mean that that particular division is going to be yours. It's probably shopworn and priced out. But the company that is selling off one division may have others that it might sell, too.

When you see a major corporation announcing a sale or closedown of a division, use your contacts to call the head of corporate development to find out if any other divisions might be for sale. You can then enter the arena at a time when corporate management might be thinking of putting something else up for sale but no one else has yet looked at it. It's critical that you carry some credibility at this time. Also, keep in mind that often these division spin-offs lead to managerial leveraged buyouts. In those cases, you may have an opportunity to tie into the management team and participate in the leveraged buyout.

Identifying the proper corporate officer to contact is critical for this approach to success. Generally a divestiture strategy will be managed by the corporate planning function, but sometimes it resides with the financial function. A few lunches invested in learning the game board can be money well spent.

Another source of divestiture intelligence is the personal acquaintance who works for a larger company and either knows of divisions for sale or knows of one in trouble. Sometimes you can get in the back door through this type of source. The lead for one of my best LBOs came when I was sitting on the train going home one night with my neighbor. He mentioned that his friend was looking for another job, and I asked why. He said that the division his friend worked for might be closed down. I asked for the name of the parent company. After four or five phone calls, I got through to the head of corporate development and was able to set up a meeting. From that point on, I used my banker as my spearhead, and I was able to close the leveraged buyout within six months.

Networking with Seasoned LBO Buyers. A third way to find deals is to get to know other leveraged buyout people. Over the years, the LBO community has evolved into an informal fraternity. A member of the fraternity can find out about deals much sooner than someone who is a novice. Get to know someone who has done several leveraged buyouts and tag along (so to speak) to obtain a piece of one leveraged buyout yourself. Often someone who has been involved in LBOs might hear of something that doesn't appeal to him—but it might be your opportunity. Offer to take anything he's not interested in and give him some action in the form of a finder's fee. In the time that I've been involved in leveraged buyouts, I've found this to be a relatively good source.

Other Sources. There are other ways to find leveraged buyouts. One is using *Standard and Poor's,* the industrial guide index to publicly held firms. Analyzing the data available from this or similar reference sources, you can evaluate the proper structure and range; you can occasionally find smaller companies that have been publicly held but for some reason can be targeted for a friendly tender offer. Usually these companies are small, are losing money, and have been poorly managed. I would caution you to keep in mind that these firms are risky prospects since, even after you succeed in negotiating a price with management, the arbitrageurs may knock out your underpinnings.

You can also find leads through information obtained at the company you're working for. Take a look at the smaller customers. Ask the accounting department which customers are generally slow payers. Many times a company that's slow to pay might be available. Using this method, I found out about one leveraged buyout that I purchased in 1976. It turned out to be a nice undertaking. While it did not grow to the degree we thought it would, we generated a 300 percent return on our investment after five years. Obviously, make sure when following this tack that you don't get into any issues of self-dealing or conflict of interest with your employer.

Yet another method you can consider is socializing with entrepreneurs who may have leads from other entrepreneurs. You can usually find this out through clubs, outings, etc. If you let the word out that you're looking for a company to buy, sometimes a lead turns up through the grapevine.

Your Number One Rule: Keep Constantly Involved

What you want to maintain at all times—and this is vital—is a constant backlog of companies that you're looking at. If you don't have a lot of options and you're looking at only one company, you may tend to compromise your predetermined target screen. When that happens, you may lose your objectivity and make a bad decision. The best deal makers are always prepared to walk away from a deal if it falls short of their standards.

I also urge you to evaluate all deals, even the ones that are not good. Don't just throw a bad deal away without probing it, although the depth of the probe will obviously be a function of your seriousness with the deal. Evaluating a deal is a good way to sharpen your teeth, a great way to learn, and a wonderful way to bide the time until a good one comes along.

If you follow this advice, you'll do more than keep things in perspective and keep yourself occupied. You'll also make a favorable impression with your lenders. Remember, you want them to see you as professional and experienced. If you are too excited, they will sense it and fear that your decision making will be based heavily on emotions. And emotion doesn't appeal to most lenders. So keep yourself involved, keep yourself interested, and pursue all avenues. To be really successful at the LBO game, you don't want to leave any stone unturned. It's not easy—but accumulating wealth seldom is. And the attainment of the objective is worth the investment.

Closing the Credibility Gap

Once you've found the deal, you've got to begin a dialog with the seller. Key to your success in this area are three elements: your ability to analyze, your ability to negotiate, and your credibility. This third element, which is critical, is often overlooked. Why should a seller deal with you rather than another potential buyer? The primary reason is that he thinks you'll get the deal done. Your initial effort with the seller, then, should not be to try to dazzle him with your intelligence but to establish your credibility. If you've never done a leveraged buyout, it's a more difficult challenge. Because it's recognized up front that you don't have the capital to fund the transaction, any hint that you don't know what you are doing will result in the door's being closed. In fact, you're essentially saying that you will be using the seller's company to provide the selling price. Obviously, when that happens the issue of funding the transaction is not totally within your control.

If you're a wealthy individual or corporation, your credibility improves—not so much because you have the cash but because you are perceived to have "decision-making ability." But if you don't have such financial resources, you'll have to gain credibility in other ways.

Linking yourself with others who are in a position of strength is an effective way for the newcomer to create credibility. You can use a banker as a reference, for instance. Ask your banker to call the prospective seller instead of your placing the call. This will help build credibility.

As mentioned earlier, in your first endeavor you might consider joining forces with established players and making your first LBO a team effort. Of course, you'll want to make sure your group presents itself as a well-organized, well-informed team, and you'll want to make sure that the chemistry of the various team members works well. Partnerships, while often essential, are not always marriages made in heaven.

The bottom line is that you will have to establish your own game plan to answer the credibility issue. My advice is to do it up front—your first chance at a given deal is often also your last.

PREPARING THE IDEAL BUSINESS PLAN

Let's assume that you've found the deal that appears to meet your standards and have opened a dialog with the seller. You now want to fine-tune your decision: Do you really want this business? If so, how can you finance it? The answer to both of these questions is rooted in the preparation of a business plan. I've seen a number of plans throughout the years—some very sophisticated, some not. And while many of these may appear to be well developed, they often fall short of being truly effective and operative in addressing the needs of both the buyer and the lender.

Most plans are loaded with marketing material and generalities depicting what will happen to the company once it is acquired. This isn't all bad, because your lenders will want to know more than what the market share is and what the product looks like. But a common thread seems to run through many of these plans that is sure to cause problems both at the negotiating table and in the future. Simply stated, this category of business plan is written just for the lender, for the purpose of raising money. These plans don't address the real business issues, and they are usually not used as a control tool once the company is purchased. Obviously this type of plan serve no ongoing purpose for the buyer. Furthermore, as lenders become more sophisticated they can spot this flaw, causing an immediate loss of credibility to the buyer.

Your total game plan should cover two specific areas: (1) the overall strategy and (2) operating tactics. The difference between the two is considerable.

The *overall strategy* consists of your long-term goals: what the company or product line will be doing within the next five years. Developing this strategy is crucial. It will keep you going in your intended direction as you progress through the development of your company. No doubt there will be times when opportunistic forces will tempt you to deviate, and a sound grand strategy will help you to stay on course unless there is a legitimate reason to change your game plan. If you've done your homework up front, changes in strategy should be minimal.

Operating tactics are generally the steps you will take that define how you will accomplish your overall strategic objectives. For example, part of the overall strategy may be the reduction of the purchase debt required for any LBO. Operating tactics might include redeployment of assets, improved turn of current assets, increased trade payables, or generation of fresh equity.

The strategy should cover not more than three objectives and should be stated in half a page or less. The tactics summary should be condensed to one page. A rambling strategic position and a loose, general statement of tactics indicate that the buyer hasn't done his homework.

The best business plan will serve three important purposes: (1) It will satisfy you that you should acquire this business. (2) It will convince the lender and the investor of your ability to operate a profit-oriented business. (3) It will become the master plan that will keep you on the right track once you acquire the company. A good business plan—or game plan—is developed for the lender, for the investor, and for you. It contains three key ingredients:

1. A heavy emphasis on the *managerial structure,* addressing any changes that may take place.
2. A good dosage of *marketing strategy,* describing how the product will be priced and sold.
3. Detailed *financial data,* both historical and projected. Planned reductions in operating expense will be identified with specificity, and planned headcount reductions will be designated by person.

These areas can be addressed in great detail, or they can be treated in more general terms. The greater the specificity, the greater the value of the plan to all parties.

Preceding the presentation of this information should be a general overview of the details that will follow. This is extremely important. Lenders, as well as investors, are inundated with all kinds of investment opportunities. It only makes sense that the simpler your approach, the more likely the lender will be to understand it; and most lenders must understand a credit before they will lend to it. A good two-page overview will let them grasp the total picture immediately rather than be forced to wade through a forest of papers. Just as important, a tight, well-structured presentation will add to your credibility.

Let's take a closer look at these three major components of your plan.

Defining the Managerial Structure

A review of the managerial structure is essential in any proposed leveraged buyout. In your operating plan, this section will include a list of key employees, with a detailed record of accomplishments relating to each of these key players. This is important because lending is based on the strength of the management team as well as the financial and/or collateral strength of the transaction. The lender is looking for performance data, not job descriptions or résumés.

The plan should also present a table of organization to enable the lender and the investor to clearly identify the key players. Also addressed in this section should be backup for key management and the compensation and incentive programs that will keep them on board. It will normally be key to the lender to see that the existing management team will remain in place, and the lenders will ask what you are doing to assure continuity. This is because the additional debt placed on the company as the result of the LBO in itself adds to the risk of the transaction, and an intelligent lender will want to assure itself that other areas of risk have been addressed and minimized.

Articulating Your Marketing Approach

Your marketing information in the game plan should be presented in terms of five general elements:

1. *The product.* Explain the product: Is the company a job shop? Are the products proprietary? Is the target a service company? Pictures of the product are helpful.
2. *Pricing the product.* Describe how the product is priced internally and how it is positioned in the marketplace. Including a

price list can be helpful. But most important, make it clear to your lenders and investors how you determine prices: Are you at the mercy of the market, in which case you must be a low-cost producer, or is price relatively insensitive, permitting you to manage your gross margin?

3. *How the product is sold in the marketplace.* Do you use representatives? Do you have a direct sales force? Do you rely heavily on distributors? Total reliance on a limited number of sales reps adds significantly to your risk unless the product is proprietary.

4. *The volume (size) of the total market.* If it's possible to arrive at the size of the total market, you can then determine the percentage of market share you hold. A market that is very large is attractive, of course, but it is also usually competitive. The higher your market share, even if the total market is small, the greater the chance that the company will be a pricing leader rather than a pricing follower.

5. *New product developments and new marketing approaches.* If you have a company that is in a turnaround situation, you may be relying heavily on new products or new marketing approaches. A lender views this approach with a jaundiced eye. The better you can document your rationale, the greater will be your credibility in this area. Keep this section short and tight—two to three pages at the most.

Financial Data: Historical and Projected

Let's turn now to the most important portion of your business plan: the financial data.

In the real world, the LBO deal boils down to whether or not the company is financially capable of servicing the debt, either by redeployment of assets or cash flow. The structure of the loan will further define additional cash flow required to retire principal. You can have the best of management and marketing programs, but if the figures do not work out, the deal will not be financeable.

With this in mind, I recommend that you place greater emphasis on the financial aspect at the beginning of your plan and then focus on the other parts of your game plan later on. One reason is that you'll develop quick feedback on whether or not the plan appears viable to the lender and investor. Also, the area that is normally most vulnerable to change as the deal progresses is financial structure, and changes should be minimal. Nothing annoys a lender more than constant changes in structure, causing changes in financing requirements.

The financial section of the business plan should be broken down into three concrete areas: (1) historical data, (2) projected data, and (3) a system to monitor actual performance against projections. This last area is critical, yet often ignored. In my experience, I've found that virtually all LBO buyers provide some degree of historical financial data and the majority also give some financial projections. However, only a minority of these buyers develop some type of follow-up to those projections, and then only a small percentage of these actually take timely corrective action if targets are missed. Unfortunately, most lenders don't determine whether monitoring and corrective actions will take place until after the loan has been funded. By then it's usually too late.

Historical Data. This data includes the historical profit and loss, the balance sheets, and the historical uses of cash. It's best to present this data in general terms, with a good overview of the company's history. Going back two or three years is helpful, but the details of this period are not vital. The past is behind us; there is nothing that can be done about it now. Historical data is most relevant when you are justifying a cost reduction program and need to compare new projected costs with historical costs. Many times, explanations of extraordinary expense can be specifically identified—for example, officers were granted large bonuses, or there was a large loss on a real estate sale. These should be noted with an asterisk at the bottom of the profit and loss or balance sheet, indicating the impact of the specific adjustment.

I'd like to stress at this point the tremendous impact that graphics can make when working with financial information. Some of the best historical budget reviews I've seen have been presented through visuals. Graphs can indicate sales volume, total cost of sales, gross margin, administrative total and selling expenses, and total net profits or losses. For the balance sheet, you can graph key ratios, accounts receivable levels, inventory levels, total fixed assets, total accounts payable, and items such as current ratios and inventory turnover. With today's microcomputer technology, a picture can, in fact, replace a thousand words.

Regarding the balance sheet, it should be remembered that the very essence of a leveraged buyout is to weaken a previously strong balance sheet. Thus, historical ratios and normal accounting ratios that have been used in the past for monitoring will generally have no validity in a leveraged buyout. You'll have a high debt level, which means that traditional debt : equity ratios are irrelevant. Ratios relating to return on assets are distorted because interest costs will be relatively high and earnings relatively low, thereby driving down the return on assets. Return on equity, on the other hand, will generally be improved. It follows, then, that many of the conventional methods used to evaluate a normal operating company are not applicable. Keep in mind that when you make a leveraged buyout, you're in essence buying time; as you gradually reduce the debt to the lender, the equity becomes more solid. The only time that the equity is meaningful is after debt has been reduced to easily manageable levels.

A financier of leveraged buyouts is most concerned with collateral coverage (if the transaction is secured) and with debt-servicing coverage (regardless of whether the transaction is secured or unsecured). Although it's important to express how profits and cash flow would be increased under your ownership, never forget that if the transaction is structured as a secured loan, you will have an uphill battle in putting the loan together if collateral is short.

Projected Financial Statement. Unsecured lenders will focus almost exclusively on cash flow. Secured lenders are interested in both cash flow and downside collateral coverage. Since they are secured, they will permit a lower debt-servicing comfort margin than will an unsecured lender. The secured lender, however, will want to see not only that the loan is collateralized going in but that it will remain that way. If assets fall short, so will the borrowing base, since secured loans are normally structured to permit borrowing of a percentage of qualified assets (e.g., up to 80 percent of accounts receivable up to 90 days from invoice date). Therefore, from both the borrower's and the lender's perspective, a balance sheet projected by month takes on added significance, particularly since the projected financial statement will look a lot different once the LBO occurs. Because this is such a critical part of the report, let's examine it in greater depth.

A set of financial projections normally encompasses profit and loss data, balance sheet data, and cash flow data. When you develop a set of projections, it is imperative that you include all three of these components. Prepare a detailed monthly profit and loss, cash flow, and balance sheet in a format compatible with your historical format. The format should not be specifically designed for the purpose of this presentation for two reasons: (1) You will be using these statements for control purposes later on, and it will be much easier to prepare a simple variance report if you use a consistent format. (2) Using a consistent format makes the deal easier for the lender to analyze.

When you prepare your projections, the starting point is to have a detailed monthly breakdown of your projected profit and loss, cash flow, and balance sheets—and to have them all tie together. You might also want to include sample breakdown calculations and some key financial ratios—accounts receivable turn, accounts payable turn, etc. And it's wise to have a few "total year" assets projections to see what the company is going to look like after a period of two or three years.

Keep in mind, though, that (1) the farther out one looks, the softer the figures, and (2) secured lenders largely discount the projections after the first year of operation. I've seen many sets of projections presented on a yearly basis for five years, but they are more meaningful to unsecured lenders than to secured lenders. The secured lender is really concentrating on the first 12 months, since that is normally the most critical period; a detailed projection by month is therefore more important to him. Also, if seasonality will cause an overadvance in any of those 12 months, this should be clearly shown; you won't see those types of swings if you're looking at a full year in a macro sense.

With the availability of personal computers, it's smart to program the computer to link the three sets of statements. That will let you make a "sensitivity analysis." A sensitivity analysis is nothing more than a series of answers to "what if" questions. What if interest rates increase to 20 percent, projected economies don't materialize, or gross margin erodes? The sensitivity analysis will answer these questions. You can develop sensitivity runs on different assumptions, but take care not to make the presentation so complex that your lenders or investors will get confused.

I've found that the best way to do this is to prepare a detailed set of projections based on a most probable occurrence, then include some condensed sensitivity runs geared to your most significant vulnerabilities. This way the lender and investor can get a quick look at what might happen if one or two occurrences take place, without having to flip through 25 pages to get to the end results. See Figure 2–1 as one approach to a 12-month base-case projection, summarizing borrowing base and borrowing need. Supporting this figure will be a 12-month profit and loss, 12-month balance sheet, and 12-month cash flow projection.

A couple of words of caution should guide you when you prepare your projections. First, keep them slightly conservative. In some financial projections I've seen, the borrower has been aggressive in projecting the advance ratios on receivables, inventory, machinery, or real estate. Based on erroneous assumptions, he makes his proposal to the seller— only to find he can't get financing. It is difficult to go back to the seller for a second bite of the apple. It is much more sound to bring your lender in as early as possible for the purpose of getting a preliminary reading on rates of advance on collateral and then structuring your proposal to the seller. Even then the lender may make changes after it analyzes the collateral, but the likelihood is that the collateral ratios initially quoted will be in the ball-park.

Another concern deals with your assumptions. Pay attention to the level of credibility your assumptions will be likely to carry, and insert only documented, credible cost reductions in your plan. You might assume, for instance, that a certain number of people (with names indicated) will be outplaced, or you might assume that a price increase will occur. This type of assumption is credible and can be documented by dollar amount. It should be contrasted with another type of assumption, which is more ephemeral. Let's look at these two kinds of assumptions more closely.

If you can determine and document that 75 people will be outplaced and their cost to the company is roughly $20,000 each per year, the resultant $1.5 million annualized savings is credible if the outplaced individuals can be identified by function. If, on the other hand, you conclude that general and administrative (G&A) expense is X percent more than industry average and a reduction to industry average will result in a $1.5 million reduction in expense, including this reduction in your projection has no credibility. Similarly, an assumption that you will get more productivity from labor by changing the work rules will not be readily accepted by a lender. It may happen, but it is based on a wish, not on hard fact.

I would suggest that in your assumptions you document the more intangible savings, but don't place them in your financial budgets. If they occur, both you and your lender are going to be pleased. If they don't occur, you haven't depended upon them. Insert only documented, credible cost reductions in your budget. Then include some accompanying text to explain the assumptions.

Contingency Plan and Corrective Action Plan. At this point in your game plan, you'll want to address the method you'll use to control the operation. Letting your lender know that you intend to monitor your performance will gain you several points. Lenders realize, of course, that even the best plans will have some areas of vulnerability. What they are truly concerned about is, assuming a glitch occurs, what you will do to put the company back on track. Indicate that monthly reports will be prepared. This will demonstrate that you realize your projections are not infallible and that you are prepared to catch problems early and correct them right away. This, in turn, will testify to your business acumen—something your lender is vitally concerned with. It's a good idea to include in your plan a sample format of a variance report (Figures 2–2 and 2–3). Of course you need to make sure that once the LBO actually takes place, documentation from that system flows back to your banker as well as to you.

I can't stress too much the importance of a corrective action plan. It's a "must" to include in your game plan, and it's a "must" to follow later on. Sadly, few managers actually employ true corrective actions before they are pushed against the wall. To show your lender you won't make that mistake, prepare a general contingency plan—a "what if" plan. Your plan should answer such questions as, "If my sales volume drops

FIGURE 2–1   "X" Company Loan Availability—Projections ($ Thousands)

Periods open*		O	N	D	J	F	M	A	M	J	J	A	S
Loan balance													
Revolving loan	$3,067	$4,144	$4,472	$4,850	$3,996	$3,890	$4,291	$4,226	$3,278	$3,262	$3,688	$4,087	$3,137
Loan availability													
A/R trade: maximum availability—80 percent	1,696	1,696	1,614	1,749	1,211	1,480	1,614	1,614	1,345	1,345	1,480	1,614	1,345
Inventory: maximum availability—50 percent	1,450	2,029	2,435	2,638	1,826	2,232	2,435	2,435	2,029	2,029	2,232	2,435	2,029
M&E (80 percent orderly liquidation)	2,000	2,000	2,000	2,000	2,000	2,000	2,000	2,000	2,000	2,000	2,000	2,000	2,000
Real estate (50 percent quick sale)	0	0	0	0	0	0	0	0	0	0	0	0	0
Other	0	0	0	0	0	0	0	0	0	0	0	0	0
Total availability	5,146	5,725	6,049	6,387	6,037	5,712	6,049	6,049	5,374	5,374	5,712	6,049	5,374
Excess (short)	2,079	1,581	1,577	1,537	2,041	1,822	1,758	1,823	2,096	2,112	2,024	1,962	2,237

"X" Company
Loan Availability

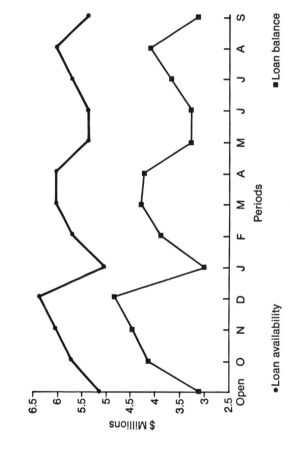

$ Millions

Periods

Open O N D J F M A M J J A S

●Loan availability   ■Loan balance

* Beginning month, October 1985.

FIGURE 2–2 **"Y" Company Year-to-Date Monthly Variance and Control Report** ($ Thousands)*

	Actual data	Flexible budget*	Dollar variance	Control budget
Gross sales.	$1,575	$1,575		$2,700
Discounts and returns.	60	59	$ (1)	101
Net sales	1,515	1,516	(1)	2,599
Cost of sales				
Material cost	1,096	1,073	(23)	1,840
Direct labor.	0	0	0	0
Manufacturing variable cost	0	0	0	0
Manufacturing factory administration.	0	0	0	0
Manufacturing fixed cost	0	0	0	0
Other expense	0	0	0	0
Total cost of sales	1,096	1,073	(23)	1,840
Gross profit.	419	443	(24)	759
Selling, general, and administration expenses				
Selling	240	187	(53)	321
Advertising	0	0	0	0
Executive.	0	0	0	0
Accounting	0	0	0	0
Personnel	0	0	0	0
General and administration	199	362	163	362
Research and development	0	0	0	0
Shipping and distribution	0	0	0	0
Total general and administration.	439	549	110	683
Other income (expense)	166	0	166	0
Operating profits before interest and taxes.	146	(106)	252	76
Interest expense	(83)	(96)	13	(96)
Net operating profits before taxes . . .	63	(202)	265	(20)
Corporate charges and organization fees	0	0	0	0
Taxes	2	(97)	(99)	(10)
Investment tax credit	0	0	0	0
Net after-tax profit	61	(105)	(166)	(10)

* Number of months: seven; period ending December 1984.
† Using actual volume to rebudget.

---

off by 10 percent, what corrective action will I take to retain a positive cash flow?" Furthermore, anticipating the problems rather than merely reacting to them permits you a more carefully thought-out course of corrective action. The axiom "Hope for the best, plan for the most likely, and anticipate the worst" is one you should live by. Incidentally, worst-case scenarios should not reflect a wholly unrealistic event; they should focus on events which could occur, but are not highly likely.

FIGURE 2–3   "Z" Company Source and Use of Cash Flow
($ Thousands)*

Assets	Beginning balance sheet (May 84)	Present balance sheet (Dec. 84)	Source and use
Cash	$ 185	$ 38	$ 147
Accounts receivable net	460	312	148
Inventory FIFO	1,320	1,393	(73)
Inventory adjustment	0	0	0
LIFO reserve	0	0	0
Other	0	10	(10)
Total current assets	1,965	1,743	
Machinery and equipment gross	212	227	(15)
Real estate	865	865	0
Accumulated depreciation	(56)	(90)	34
Intangible assets	49	45	4
Total assets	$3,035	$2,790	
Liabilities and net worth			
Accounts payable	$ 408	$ 125	(283)
Accruals	225	116	(109)
Insurance accrual	0	0	0
Pension accrual	0	0	0
ABL loans	0	165	165
Other	61	61	0
Total current liabilities	694	467	
Long-term debt	0	0	0
Other	988	953	(35)
Tax accrual	0	0	0
Deferred credits	10	10	0
Total long-term debt	998	963	
Net worth:			
Capital stock and surplus	75	75	0
Paid-in surplus	1,226	1,226	0
Earned surplus	42	68	26
Total net worth	1,343	1,369	
Total liabilities and net worth	$3,035	$2,799	

* Period ending December 1984.

One of the advantages of dealing with an asset-based lender in financing an LBO is that the target's profits are not as critical to the lender as are cash flow and collateral coverage. You obviously must have good operating profits to generate a consistent cash flow to retire your debt. But because the asset-based lender has collateral, in the event you suffer a heavy loss, he can afford to ride with you for a longer period of time—provided you are following a solid game plan and soundly managing your assets to conserve cash. Even the secured lender will quickly lose patience, however, if corrective actions are not taken to turn around the situation and get the company back on track. The contingency plan facilitates these corrective actions.

MAKING THE BIG MOVE: PRESENTING THE PLAN

Let's assume that you have prepared the business plan and concluded you want to make the deal. Now you must present the plan to your lender to get financing. This presentation can be a winning one if you pay attention to some specifics. To start, don't get bogged down with details at first. Remember what it is you want to accomplish in the initial presentation: You want to review the plan in general and address the basic issues. To throw the whole presentation in front of your lender will just confuse him. The details will come later, prior to funding, and then you'll need to have answers. But don't waste your time talking about line items initially. Walk your lender through the overview, sense how much he can absorb, and don't lose him. If necessary, wait until subsequent meetings to get into the sensitivity analysis.

If you're fortunate enough, however, to have found an intelligent lender—and they are relatively rare—your first meeting can cover the entire business plan, contingencies and all. The name of the game is complete disclosure, but fed at a level the lender can understand. Don't deal in half-truths, and don't color the picture to entice the lender. You'll end up regretting it.

Your game plan should be outlined and presented in a professional manner. Make it easy to read, quick to comprehend, and allow the lender to pose questions that you can address specifically. Most people try to have all the questions answered in their plan. But if you can demonstrate the ability to come up with those answers during the meeting, you'll make a favorable impression and will have kept your report concise. And don't forget a rule that's been proven over and over: the more visual aids you use in the game plan, the better.

Another important consideration is who should present the plan. I've found that it's best to have the management people present it, usually the one or two key players in the LBO. It's not beneficial to have every interested party present at the first meeting—the lawyers and accountants can attend later meetings but not the first. Their fees will be high enough without overusing them. And if you're not in a position to answer some of the business questions that are posed, don't bluff. The stakes are too high.

Finally, be sure to give the lender and investor time to read the game plan prior to your meeting. Submit it to each at least a day in advance so they can review it, test it, and come up with questions. The purpose of the first meeting is to determine if you have the basis for a deal. Don't come up with a preordained financing structure; that will be accomplished at a later date. You should know the purchase price and the amount of equity you can raise. Whether you need additional debt support beyond what the lender will provide is a subject you can discuss later—if the framework of the deal is sound.

Chapter 3

The Seller's View of a Leveraged Buyout

James Long
Mark H. Friedman

The other chapters of this book focus primarily on LBOs from a buyer's perspective. But without a seller, there can be no buyer. We'd like to share with you some of the seller's thinking in structuring an LBO.

In what has been one of the larger asset redeployments in the history of U.S. industry, American Can Company has transformed itself from an old-line manufacturer of cans and paper products into a diversified organization with activities in financial services, direct mail marketing and speciality retailing, high-performance plastics packaging, and state-of-the-art metal can production. By replacing low-growth, capital-intensive businesses with service or working capital-intensive businesses, American Can has eliminated many factors that produced earnings volatility over the last few years and has set the stage for rapid growth in higher margin activities. The asset redeployment involved 27 divestitures of from $1 million to $430 million. Over the last 10 years, American Can Company has completed 90 transactions approximating $2 billion in value. Of these transactions, 14 have been LBOs, 13 on the sell side and one on the buy side, including international transactions in Australia, Canada, and Germany.

The Corporate Mergers & Acquisitions (M&A) group, as part of the chairman's strategic work committee, participated in developing the above asset redeployment plan. One of the results of the plan was the September 30, 1982, establishment of a $247 million pretax reserve

($175 million after taxes), for the disposition of nonstrategic businesses. Once the plan was approved by the board of directors, the Mergers and Acquisitions group was charged with its implementation.

The objective in each sale has been to sell nonstrategic businesses for full value to qualified buyers who will afford the employees of the divested business unit a good opportunity to further their careers. As part of the sale decision, the M&A group assesses the marketability and anticipates the price range for the business unit. In making this assessment, the M&A group acts much like an in-house investment bank in looking at comparable transactions. In those instances in which it appears likely that a sale may well involve an LBO, the M&A group will do an internal valuation of what an LBO structure can finance.

In most instances, the M&A group will also look at alternatives to the sale of the business as a whole, including a sale of components or liquidation. A sale of components will often allow American Can to optimize value, as well as afford the greatest future opportunity for the greatest number of employees. Liquidation values enable the establishment of a baseline value for the most difficult turnaround situations. In a few instances this has convinced potential purchasers of the minimum acceptable purchase price and has, fortunately, enabled American Can to consummate certain difficult transactions at premiums to liquidation value while avoiding the agony of actual liquidation.

The prime consideration for prospective buying groups is determining the seller's view of values. If the seller is not realistic in viewing economic value versus historic investment or replacement cost, a transaction is unlikely. Our announced reserve action stimulated interest of corporations and LBO groups, as it indicated recognition of economic value versus book value upon divestiture of the nonstrategic businesses. LBO groups should be wary of involvement with corporate sellers who have not recognized a prospective loss on a divestiture, where the economic value is substantially less than the historic value.

Once we have the green light to sell, we get our internal house in order and prepare an offering memorandum and a marketing program prior to soliciting potential buyers. To assure business continuity, we normally enter into change-of-control agreements with key employees of the business unit. This gives them an incentive to cooperate with the sales efforts and to assess objectively their future opportunities, despite the natural anxiety arising from the prospective sale. Many LBOs have provided entrepreneurial opportunities to key management through equity participation in the buyout.

The corporate marketing effort focuses on logical and strategic buyers. We contact prospective buyers directly, with limited use of the services of investment bankers. When we publicly announced our major corporate restructuring in fall 1982, many potential suitors, investment bankers, and other financial service organizations contacted us to ascertain what opportunities existed. In most situations, the LBO transactions evolved after it was ascertained that a sale to a financially strong strategic buyer was not practicable. Our experience indicates that an LBO group will not generally outbid a financially strong corporate strategic buyer, which will usually obtain synergistic cost and revenue benefits from the acquisition.

The successful LBO groups have approached us and established credibility with us directly or through intermediaries—such as commercial and investment bankers or public accounting firms. In short, the successful LBO groups have to search and uncover the corporate opportunities; generally the corporation does not seek them out, but instead has to grade and select among competing groups.

When approached by an LBO group, we qualify its ability to close the prospective transaction and operate successfully postclosing. Thus we look at its track record in other deals, financial resources, negotiating ability, industry knowledge, management experience, and entrepreneurial skills. This is the initial critical point for prospective LBO groups—convincing the corporate seller that they can, first, *close* the transaction and, second, *operate* successfully. The LBO group has to establish its credibility at the outset; otherwise it will not get beyond the first meeting.

Prior to approaching a corporate seller, LBO groups should have lined up prospective lending institutions who will articulate a willingness to consider financing the transaction. Corporate sellers will want to talk directly to the proposed lending institution to judge the group's ability to finance the transaction before proceeding with negotiations.

The corporate seller will also try to ascertain the buying group's personal financial resources and willingness to commit those resources to providing the initial equity capital as well as supporting future operating needs if cash flow problems should develop postclosing. It is not inappropriate for an LBO group to represent its financial resources and the extent to which it is willing to commit them. Such a representation enables the seller to prioritize competing LBO groups.

Most buyers say, "Why do *you* care, if you've got *your* cash at closing?" The answer is twofold. In the first instance, many corporations are concerned about a broader responsibility to communities, business relationships, and the future of the employees affected by the sale. A given transaction is one of many transactions for the corporation. If businesses sold go downhill, jeopardizing communities and former employees' careers and lives, then the seller's ongoing operations and potential future transactions will be negatively impacted as current employees become concerned about their future. The second part of the response is that, while the seller gets its money at closing, it expects to keep it. If a business is sold in an LBO and the buyer does not achieve its financial expectations, under certain circumstances outlined in Chapter 9 of this book the seller risks claims in bankruptcy against the proceeds from the sale.

In evaluating the buyer's transactional qualifications, the seller will look at prior deals or the qualifications of the buying group's negotiator, who is typically an attorney, investment banker, or deal maker with specific experience in LBOs. No one should be interested in dry runs, as the goal is to close the transaction. LBOs are complex legal and financial transactions. For people interested in doing LBOs, it is good advice to line up experienced professionals as part of the team prior to approaching a prospective candidate, to present the group in the most positive fashion.

Professional and entrepreneurial managerial skills also need to be demonstrated. When the buyout group includes members of existing management, it is easier for the seller to assess the buyer's ability to operate successfully and protect the seller's interests regarding employees and future claims against the proceeds from sale. If the buying group does not include existing management or existing management is not attuned to operating under conditions of high financial leverage, then it is necessary for the buyer to convince the seller that it has the managerial resources and experience to do so.

Having gotten over the initial hurdle of convincing the corporate seller that it can finance and negotiate the transaction and operate successfully, the LBO group, during the course of negotiations to the point of closing, must confirm the initial judgments by its actions. The months from initiation to closing represent a period of getting to know the buyer; the time offers an opportunity for the corporate seller to validate its initial judgment. If during the process of negotiation, financing, due diligence, and business planning, the prospective buyer is found wanting, the corporate seller has to assess the risks of proceeding to close.

Having qualified an LBO group as a prospective bidder, the next step is the negotiation itself. The LBO group is often competing against similar groups as well as against management. If existing management meets the qualifications of an LBO, it will normally have preference over other LBO groups. Since LBOs have become commonplace and use similar financing arrangements, the successful bidder will normally pay the most that can be successfully financed.

In our largest transaction, which was several hundred million dollars, the winning difference was the buyer's $20 million of equity, which the management-led group did not have, as well as the quality and marketability of the securities taken back as part of the transaction. In that instance, we (as the seller) determined what an LBO group could afford to pay, and the two bidders, supported by investment bankers, independently arrived at the same valuation. The lesson is, if you want to have the winning bid, be prepared to offer the most that a sophisticated LBO analysis indicates can be financed. Secondly, if seller financing is part of the deal, be assured that the quality, liquidity, and real value of the paper will be a major consideration to the seller.

Once your bid has been accepted, you have to concurrently obtain financing commitments, conduct due diligence, prepare a detailed business plan, evaluate and assuage management and enlist their support, and negotiate a definitive agreement.

As a seller, we place a short fuse on the financing commitment: one month for smaller transactions and two months for large transactions. We also subject the financing commitment to our approval in order to have comfort that the business will have sufficient capital to operate successfully post closing, again to protect our proceeds and the welfare of employees. To this end, we have at times found ourselves in the unusual position of assisting the buyer in negotiating with his lenders to obtain more flexible financing terms.

Having gotten past the hurdles of qualifying the LBO bidder, negotiating the deal, and obtaining the financing commitments, the LBO (from the corporate seller's perspective) takes on the characteristics of other divestitures through closing.

For the benefit of prospective LBO participants, we would like to recapitulate the key points to be considered when dealing with a corporate seller:

1. Aggressively solicit the corporate seller to develop opportunities.
2. Ascertain if competing actual bidders are likely to include well-capitalized strategic buyers.
3. Determine economic value and compare to the seller's perceived value. Especially, qualify the corporate seller in turnaround situations. Has it written down, or is it willing to write down, the value of the business for sale at its economic value.
4. The LBO group must qualify itself to the corporate seller at the outset. It must convincingly articulate its ability to close the transaction and operate successfully postclosing. Closing qualifications include:
   a. Sufficient equity.
   b. Established relationships with financial sources.
   c. Transactional experience from prior deals or experienced advisors.

Operating qualifications include:

- *a.* Entrepreneurial and management skills.
- *b.* Industry knowledge.
- *c.* Availability of contingency funds for negative deviations from the business plan.

5. Be sensitive to the seller's contingent liabilities and bankruptcy risks.
6. If you want to succeed, bid the most that can successfully be financed in a competitive situation. If the seller is assisting in financing, the quality, value, and liquidity of the paper could be determinative in the decision to proceed.
7. The successful LBO group has to reinforce continuously the seller's positive impression of the buyer's qualifications by its conduct through closing.
8. Evaluate and determine the business unit key management's continuing role and potential equity participation.

Part II

Financing

Chapter 4

Seeking Financing: An Overview

Let's assume that you've found your deal and you've prepared your business plan. Your number one priority is to obtain financing. Where should you go to get the deal done?

Remember that the financial marketplace is no different from a shopping mall: If you go to the right shop you can probably find what you need, but finding that shop can be a frustrating experience. Also remember that providers of funds are in business to generate a profit. The greater their perceived downside risk, the greater will be the upside benefits they will demand. Each provider has established certain criteria that are consistent with its concept of an appropriate risk: reward ratio.

Financing is normally obtained from one of the two following sources:

- Secured lenders.
- A consortium of banks, insurance companies, LBO funds and venture capitalists combining to provide unsecured financing.

For each of these sources, the entrepreneur has two primary alternatives:

- He can seek to package the financing himself.
- He can work through a broker or loan packager to arrange the financing.

Our experience is that if the funding is to be secured, the entrepreneur should invest the time and seek the financing himself rather than going through a broker. The broker adds nothing of substance to the deal; what he does add is an ability to direct the buyer to the right lending source. The buyer can do this himself with a little investment in time. Furthermore, his CPA will probably be able to provide this service at a cost considerably lower than the brokerage fee.

If the deal, however, is to be structured on an unsecured basis, there is a great degree of sophistication required in determining the appropriate amount of venture capital, subordinated debt, and senior debt that can be carried. Unless the buyer is extremely knowledgeable and experienced, he will not be able to propose the optimal financing package. Therefore, if the deal is to be structured as an unsecured credit, the buyer should normally work through a professional packager, such as a corporate finance department of a commercial or investment bank. The starting point, then, should be to determine whether the deal can be structured as a secured credit. We will discuss this in some more detail shortly, but first let us share some additional observations about financing.

It's important to remember that when you are arranging the financing, you are seeking to resolve four conflicting alternatives, and you must trade off between them.

First and most important, you want to get the deal done. The old story of the butcher who has underpriced the market on hamburger—but is out of hamburger—is applicable. The cost of financing is immaterial if the financier can't deliver.

Second, you want to minimize the amount required to service your debt. Since this is a function of interest rate and mandatory principal repayments, you will normally seek the lowest rate and the longest amortization term available.

Third, you want to maximize your upside potential. Your primary objective in making the acquisition is to accumulate wealth. You therefore want to retain as large a piece of the deal as possible in order to maximize your upside gain.

Fourth, you want to have a financing source that will adequately understand your problems and the business, will be supportive when appropriate, and won't panic when problems do arise. In short, the buyer seeks to get the deal done quickly and cheaply with no dilution and with a comfort factor. The financing source, on the other hand, wishes to make sure that it has an appropriate risk : reward payback; the greater the degree of its perceived risk, the greater will be its insistence on a piece of the action.

The trade-offs between these conflicting goals are often difficult. While your first priority is to get the deal done, a good financing source can be helpful in identifying risks that you may have overlooked. The optimal trade-off between downside coverage, upside gain, and comfort with the financing source varies with each deal.

The less complicated the structure, the easier it is to obtain financing. A secured deal normally involves three players—the buyer, the seller, and the financing source. An unsecured deal adds to the complexity by adding different levels of financing—including senior unsecured debt, subordinated debt, and venture capital—all normally coming from different sources. Because of its relative simplicity, a secured deal can normally be done more quickly than an unsecured deal. Furthermore, it will normally leave a greater proportionate share of equity with the buyer. Thus there is a greater upside gain to the buyer in developing this type of structure. On the other hand, in terms of debt servicing, a secured deal will often have a higher stated interest rate than an unsecured deal. An offset to this is that the secured deal can often be structured with minimal fixed amortization. And because the lender has collateral, it may tend to swing a little more in the event of a temporary downturn in the cash flow.

In summary, if it's available, secured financing is probably the route you should seek first on most transactions, although as the deal gets larger the likelihood of adequate collateral coverage decreases—particularly if the purchase price involves a significant premium over book value. As you make more deals, you'll be able to define the transaction that clearly does not qualify for secured lending; but as a general rule, start with a bias toward secured structuring and go to an unsecured structure only as a second alternative. The following two guidelines should help you determine whether financing should be secured or unsecured:

- *Size.* The smaller the transaction, the more likely that the appropriate financing source should be a secured lender. If the transaction involves less than $20 million of financing, it's often difficult to pique the interest of the mezzanine financing and venture capital communities. If the deal gets larger, it may still be properly housed in a secured lending institution, but there is also a greater likelihood the necessary players in an unsecured structuring can be attracted.
- *Collateral coverage.* The closer the relationship of liquidating values of acquired assets to the total financing need, the greater the likelihood of finding a secured financing source. Conversely, the greater the premium over book and the less tangible the asset base, the greater the difficulty in finding a secured lending source. As we will discuss shortly, secured lenders will stretch on occasion, but those who stretch the farthest will require some additional payment for their incremental risk.

When you're financing a leveraged buyout, remember that the financing package must include not only the acquisition financing but also a refinancing of the company's existing debt structure and provision for adequate working capital. It's reasonable to assume that all of the company's long-term debt, including interest-attractive industrial revenue bonds (IRBs), must be refinanced, since the acquisition will probably result in a breach of one or more of the covenants contained in the loan indenture. Thus the amount of financing required will always be greater than the acquisition financing itself. It is not reasonable to assume that existing lenders will remain in the credit on their present basis with a significantly degraded corporate financial statement.

We touched earlier on the difference between balancing the downside effect of heavier debt-servicing obligations against the increased shareholder dilution caused by the infusion of increased permanent capital. In determining the cost of the financing package, one should look at both of these factors. A little more explanation is in order.

In analyzing fixed interest cost, the buyer has to remember that the rate structure, stated alone, is only one element. A lender will often quote rates in terms of a combination of an interest rate on funds employed, a closing fee, a fee for providing the credit facility, an unused line fee covering the difference between the amount of borrowing and the amount of the maximum facility, and perhaps an auditing fee, a servicing fee, and a myriad of other items. Every lender states its charges differently. It's important for the buyer to analyze all elements of cost in determining what his actual effective interest cost will be. A prime + 2 financing charge on a $10 million facility can be more expensive than a prime + 3 charge—if the former also charges a $100,000 closing fee and a $100,000-per-year facility fee.

Although it's true, as we'll discuss later, that cheaper is not necessarily better—remember that generally the most critical elements to you are getting the deal done and continued servicing after the deal is on the books—all cost components should be taken into account to determine financing costs. You can determine whether you are willing to pay X percent more for the additional service you'll be getting from Company A rather than Company B, but that decision can be made only after you've analyzed all the criteria to determine how large "X" really is.

Looking at the other end of the equation, on the upside the most expensive money one can find is that from the venture capitalists. While their equity interest may incur no fixed interest expense or debt-servicing requirement on their investment, a good venture capitalist will seek a relatively high compound return on its investment, commensurate with the risk it is taking.

Table 4–1 is an oversimplification, but is should give the reader a

TABLE 4–1   Type of Financing Partners

Type of financing	Principal source	Form of financing	Target rate of return
Asset-based financing.	Asset-based lenders, e.g., banks, industrial, and commercial finance companies.	Secured floating-rate financing, availability based on percent of current and fixed assets.	1–4 percent spread over prime plus administration fee; sometimes includes equity kicker in form of warrants, cheap common stock, or percent of cash flow if credit requires collateral stretch.
Senior bank debt.	Banks.	Generally unsecured, but occasionally secured, (1) looking to cash flow as source of repayment and (2) requiring greater underlying dollar equity base than asset-based lenders.	Commitment fee plus 1–2½ percent spread over prime; rarely take equity kicker.
Fixed-rate senior and subordinated debt sold as a "strip" to same purchasers.	Insurance companies, pension funds mezzanine buyout funds.	Unsecured fixed-rate debt coupled with equity participation in the form of partial convertibility, warrants, or cheap common stock.	20–35 percent compound return on investment from rate plus equity.
Preferred stock or subordinated debt.	Venture capitalists, principally venture subsidiaries of bank holding companies, mezzanine buyout funds, and some insurance companies.	Fixed-rate preferred stock or subordinated debt which is usually redeemable and coupled with equity participation in form of partial convertibility, warrants, or cheap common stock.	35–50 percent compound return on investment from rate plus equity.
Common stock.	Leveraged buyout specialists and funds, venture capitalists, ESOPs.	Common stock with no current return.	50 percent compound return on investment entirely from equity.

relative idea of effective rates and all-inclusive costs of particular types of fundings. When reviewing this table, please keep in mind that it assumes the venture is successful and in fact the participants participate in their upside gains. The relative costs to the company and to the shareholders of an equity investment are quite different, and the ongoing interest expense of debt obviously impacts a company's chance for success more negatively than does an equity investment.

With this background data, let's focus in Chapter 5 on the criteria secured lenders use in determining whether or not to finance your particular transaction.

Chapter 5

Seeking Financing: The Secured Leveraged Buyout

WHO ARE THE PLAYERS?

Secured lending, commercial finance, and *asset-based lending* are all terms used interchangeably to indicate a lender who will focus its credit decision on collateral coverage and ability to service interest rather than on financial strength and ability to amortize principal. But there are different levels of secured lenders, with different credit criteria. It's useful to recognize the players and the capabilities of each.

Picture a credit continuum, if you will, similar to the following:

$$\longleftarrow \hspace{5cm} \longrightarrow$$

100 percent collateral	100 percent cash flow

At the theoretical left-hand side would be lenders that insist on being collateralized but care nothing about the client's viability. At the theoretical right-hand side would be lenders that rely exclusively on the borrower's cash flow, with a total disregard of collateral values. Each lender fits somewhere on the continuum, but often it is difficult for the borrower to identify the position; in fact, sometimes the lender itself has difficulty in identifying its target qualify range.

It's a fair generalization to state that the small commercial finance companies tend toward the left and the larger money center banks tend toward the right, with the larger finance companies and most regional banks tending somewhere toward the center. Table 5–1 describes the most likely players for different loan profiles. The listing is not gospel. Your CPA or attorney will probably know the most likely

---

TABLE 5–1   **Leveraged Buyouts: Loan and Player Profiles**

Loan profile	*Most probable player*
Adequate collateral, poor cash flow, no clear turnaround plan; game plan is to redeploy assets.	Small commercial finance company.
Adequate collateral, poor cash flow, turnaround plan well documented.	Commercial finance companies, secured lending units of sophisticated banks.
Adequate collateral, good cash flow.	Every secured lender.
Poor collateral, weak cash flow, no clear turnaround plan; game plan is to redeploy assets.	Good luck!
Poor collateral, weak cash flow, turnaround plan well documented.	Limited number of sophisticated lenders.
Poor collateral, strong cash flow.	Money center banks, regional banks if borrower has proven track record.

---

financing source in your community for the particular transaction involved. But it should be useful as a guide. When the game plan of the acquisition is liquidation, you are less likely to find a money center bank willing to rely totally on asset redeployment than a finance company. And when it is accompanied by a solid cash flow, you are more likely to get a higher advance on collateral from a money center bank than from a lender who wants to define its downside risk.

This differentiation points to the fact that asset-based lending has developed into two different product groups. There are asset-based lenders who look to assets for downside protection and will adhere closely to liquidating values; and there are those who will advance on fair market valuation (or even higher valuations), recognizing that their downside is not totally covered and that they have a built-in exposure but relying on the borrower's cash flow to support the credit decision. Both of these schools of thought have advantages and disadvantages to the borrower.

Old-School Secured Lending

The old-school secured lending philosophy is based on the premise that since the borrower does not merit unsecured credit, the credit rationale must be based on downside collateral coverage. These lenders analyze collateral from a liquidating perspective, even though they may not believe the liquidation will actually occur. Rates of advance on collateral will be based on the ratio of accounts receivable that will be realized if the company's operation is terminated; inventories will be valued at a quick sale value with no credence given to converting work in process to more salable finished goods; machinery and equipment will be valued at net value realizable from an auction sale after expenses; and real estate value will be based on the most likely price available within four to six months of offering. Contracts and other intangibles will normally have little if any value.

An old-school secured lender may overadvance on collateral, but a good one will always start with the downside coverage. Its loan documentation will permit reduction in rates of advance at its discretion; overadvances will generally be limited to short-term periods; and such overadvances will be made only if short-term cash flow projections support the fact that they can be repaid.

The disadvantage to the borrower of this type of lending is obvious: Available leverage will not be as great as with a more aggressive lending formula. There is therefore less chance of getting the deal done.

The advantages, however, can be even greater. Since the lender is collateralized, it can ride with a temporary downswing without panicking. And in the vast majority of leveraged buyouts, there is at least some temporary downswing. If the worst case occurs and the company fails, there is little likelihood that the borrower's personal guarantee will have to be called upon if the loan is adequately collateralized by the business assets—the guarantor and the lender have identical interests, and a game plan to solve emerging problems is relatively easy to agree upon. Furthermore, since the secured lender has minimized its downside risk, it normally will not be entitled to a significant upside benefit, such as an upside rate sharing or equity participation.

The "Corporate Finance" Secured Lender

This school of though relies primarily on the company's projected cash flow. The approach can range from advancing unrealistically high levels on the borrower's assets to making a large overadvance which can only be repaid through successful operations or subsequent placement of "junk bonds." From the standpoint of getting the deal done, this type of approach is often highly desirable to the borrower. From the perspective of living with the lender after the loan is closed, however, there is significantly greater risk to the borrower. Perhaps the lender is so exposed that it will be willing to rely totally on the borrower to bail it out, and increase its loans even in the event of trouble. More likely, however, in the event of a downturn the lender will attempt to force the loan down. The promoter in this type of structure is taking a significantly greater risk in the venture's continued success, since in the event of downside it's probable not only that his guarantee will be called upon but that he'll have to make good on it through assets not related to his investment in the company.

Most of the secured lenders who are structuring LBOs are members of the National Commercial Finance Association, the trade association of asset-based financiers which is headquartered in Manhattan. It can be a good screen to cull out some players who call themselves secured lenders but aren't really actively engaged in the game. When making a decision, however, it's important to remember that the ability of a secured lender to structure a deal is a function both of the institutional strength of the lender and of the individuals representing the lender.

Make sure you get involved not only with an institution that you feel comfortable with, but with an individual who can get the job done. It's not always easy to identify these individuals—and it is often not a function of title. There is a natural inclination to try to go as high in an organization as possible to reach a decision maker, but generally the seniors will bounce the grunt work back to the juniors and involve themselves only at the actual decision-making time. You will also find that some organizations use the team approach, requiring the involvement of a number of specialists (each working on a particular aspect of the transaction), while some use an individual approach.

A general rule is that you'll want to interface primarily with one individual, but the more resources that individual has available to him to work on specific areas of the acquisition, the more probable he will deliver a sound structure. The best course of action is to check within the local community to find out which players have the best reputation—not only for structuring a deal but for working with you after the deal is booked, the euphoria has passed, and the hard work is upon you.

WHAT YOUR LENDER SHOULD EXPECT OF YOU

Assuming the secured lender has done his background check and determined that you are the type of individual that he feels comfortable in dealing with, your meetings with the secured creditor are designed to answer three points:

- Do you know what you are buying?
- Are you willing to go at risk on the credit?
- Can you arrange enough funds to cover the difference between the combined payout and working capital needs of the company and the amount the secured lender is willing to lend?

Let's look at each of these in a little more depth.

Do You Know What You Are Buying?

To a secured lender, upside gain is nice, but downside risk coverage is critical. The whole dialogue with the secured lender, therefore, will be focused initially on what the company will look like immediately after the leveraged buyout takes place, what your management game plan is, and what your contingency plans are if vulnerabilities should become real. Are there risks of some particular company strength (that has been critical to the company's success in the past) expiring when the deal is closed?

The first set of issues relate to sales. Personal relationships between vendors and their customers are often difficult to identify, but the buyers certainly should know who controls which customer relationships, what the likelihood might be of the control people leaving, and what the likelihood of losing the customer might be, should that occur.

Assuming you have satisfied the lender that you understand the sales vulnerabilities, the next set of issues will relate to production. What are labor relations like, and what is the possibility of a strike? How much has to be plowed into production facilities, and over what period of time, to keep the company a competitive producer?

Looking at total operating expenses, if you projected a staff take-down, to what extent have you detailed it and how realistic will the new cost structure be? What will be the impact of the additional interest load, and how sensitive to changes in the prime rate will it be? There is also the item of allocated general and administrative expense that most buyers cavalierly assume will be eliminated after the buyout is completed; however, there are often some services that are actually rendered by the home office for this allocated expense, and the question has to be answered to what extent these services would force additional expenditures if they were provided in house or by a third-party vendor.

It's obvious that this question list isn't all-inclusive. The purpose of the exercise is for you to explain to the lender that you understand the business, you understand the risks, and you're prepared to cope with them. If a question comes up that you can't answer, the lender would rather hear you say that you haven't addressed that issue than to have you attempt to bluff your way through it. Remember, you are establishing two things with the lender: your knowledge base and your credibility. No one knows all the answers to all the conceivable questions. Although one would clearly prefer to deal with a buyer who is both totally credible and totally knowledgeable, if there is a trade-off, an intelligent lender will pick credibility every day.

To What Extent Are You Willing to Go at Risk?

In the old days of leveraged buyouts, individuals could often put deals together with no equity and with nothing more than a guarantee against perpetrating acts of fraud. This was possible when purchases were made at deep discounts and the lender felt perfectly comfortable with the collateral.

As prices have escalated over the years, not only have discounts become relatively infrequent but significant premiums are often involved in leveraged buyouts. The decision is tougher for the lender because it may be asked to stretch on the collateral or the cash flow. It wants to know that you're going to be around to help in the event of trouble. Normally it will require some equity investment just to make sure you have an interest up front. But in the event of a downside, that equity investment can disappear in a hurry. The lender will also, therefore, normally want some type of assurance that you won't toss in the keys if trouble develops. This assurance is usually expressed in the form of a guarantee which may take one of three shapes:

1. A full guarantee of payment, under which the buyer unequivocably agrees to guarantee the total obligation of the borrower.
2. A full performance guarantee, under which the buyer unequivocably agrees to make good to the lender any shortfall, after a certain time frame is permitted to allow the lender to liquidate the collateral, with the guarantee being limited to the shortfall.
3. A limited performance guarantee, which both limits the maximum dollar exposure of the guarantor and limits the ability of the lender to call on the guarantee without first having proceeded against the collateral to realize the proceeds from it. Normally the limited performance guarantee will be limited to perhaps a 120-day grace period, and the lender will normally insist on a waiver stipulating that it need not have exhausted its legal remedies before proceeding against the guarantee. Absent such a waiver, calling on the guarantee can be deferred for years as the legal process slowly grinds along, and this risk is normally not acceptable to a lender.

Whatever the form of the guarantee, the secured lender is normally looking for one thing in the event of trouble: the cooperation of the borrower in maximizing the value of the collateral. To the extent there is a guarantee, both the guarantor and the secured lender are in an identical posture; without a guarantee, the buyer will often treat the lender at arm's length since he has no real interest in whether the lender gets out whole or not, except for a possible taint to his reputation if a loss to the lender results.

Every lender has a different appetite for the different guarantee alternatives. My personal bias, for example, is for limited performance guarantees, but in an amount that makes it significant to the borrower. For example, a $250,000 guarantee on a $10 million loan from an individual who has a net worth of $500,000 is probably more realistically collectible than a full $10 million guarantee from that same individual. On the other hand, such a guarantee from an individual who has a multimillion dollar net worth may be so insignificant that it does not assure the desired cooperation.

The issue of a guarantee often arises when there are multiple buyers or when the management group is acquiring a rather small piece of a publicly held company. The extent to which an individual institution is willing to waive the guarantee is a judgment factor; but normally, if the management group will end up with a significant piece of the action, the key players will be asked to give (at a minimum) either several or joint and several limited performance guarantees.

To What Extent Can You Cover the Financing Gap?

The third set of issues the lender is attempting to resolve relates to what the financing needs of the target company will be and the extent to which they can be covered by collateral ratios with which the lender feels comfortable. To the extent there is a gap between the two figures, it can be filled from the following sources:

1. A combination of equity or subordinated debt supplied by investors.
2. A note taken back by the seller, with repayment consistent with the company's cash flow.
3. An overadvance on collateral by the lender.

To the extent the lender is asked to come up with an overadvance, the buyer can expect to pay some premium. If the overadvance can be cured from the company's cash flow in a relatively short period of time, the premium may be minimal. If, on the other hand, it's a significant amount and the method of repayment is from long-term earnings, a subsequent stock or "junk bond" issue, or a redeployment of assets, the premium will often be significant and will be in the form of some type of interest kicker or equity kicker. The amount of the premium will also be a function of the track record of the buyer and the overall condition of the target company after the leveraged buyout is completed. The point is that the intelligent buyer will understand in his negotiations that he must somehow repay the lender for a perceived incremental risk.

WHAT YOU SHOULD EXPECT FROM YOUR LENDER

It may well be true that there are a number of potential buyers seeking leveraged acquisition financing who don't fit the qualifications for a particular lender. The fact that a particular buyer fails a given lender's credit screen may be a reflection on the buyer—or it may equally reflect on the lender. Lenders are like running shoes: The fact that they are highly rated and well acclaimed does not mean that they will properly fit your foot. While the lender might well be paying your cost of admission, you are contributing to his salary—and you are entitled to be serviced by a lender who meets your qualifications.

It's an unfortunate fact of life in the credit business that a number of lenders promise what they can't deliver. Sometimes they give you a positive indication because of ignorance; at other times they deliberately tell half-truths to keep the buyer on the hook on the assumption that the shorter his time frame and the fewer his options, the greater the likelihood that the lender can bait and switch by restructuring the credit initially offered to the buyer. Unfortunately the problem is not always an institutional one. There are many cases where an overly aggressive sales representative of the lender winks at company policy in order to get the deal. This is particularly true in institutions that pay a commission to their business development people based on their productivity. I would suggest, then, that your first starting point is to check to see that the institution has a reputation for delivering what it says it will, and that the individual you are dealing with within that institution has a similar reputation.

Having done that, you should then determine that you're going to be getting what you paid for. In promoting an LBO, you're looking to a financing source for two things: its ability to get the deal done and its willingness to stick with you after the deal is done, to provide counsel and advice where appropriate, and to have some staying power if things don't go totally according to plan. You therefore have to determine what you are buying for the money you are paying. If you're getting a quick yes and an even quicker trigger finger in the event of adversity, there is no interest rate low enough to compensate you for the additional risk you are going to be assuming.

On the other hand, it's not realistic to assume that you'll find a lender who will stay with you, come hell or high water, if you proceed to run the operation into the ground after the acquisition is completed. The best balance is probably a lender who has taken the time to understand your business fully, who understands your business plan, and who has the capacity to counsel you after the acquisition is completed to make sure you are sensitive to the concerns it may have. It does not take a basket full of brain power to congratulate you when you show a profit or tap you on the wrist when you show a loss; it does, however, take some understanding to realize what is really happening to your cash flow and which way the variables in the business are driving it.

If you find a lender that has the capacity to get the deal done in a reasonable period of time, has the desire to work with you in understanding the business and the business plan, has a commitment to track the business plan after the fact, and has the patience to stick with you if you are operating under a sound business premise but suffering a temporary setback, you have found the best of all worlds. And if you can find such a lender without having to pay an equity kicker, at an effective interest rate that your cash flow indicates you can support, you should not look elsewhere to try to save that extra half a point.

Of course, as the deals get stronger and less creativity is required on the part of the lender, you are entitled to a lower rate to reflect the lower risk the lender is assuming. In today's market, however, the risks are increasing, not decreasing, and your protection against the lender is not in the documentation—which is invariably sided toward the lender—but in the working relationship you establish with it.

Chapter 6

Seeking Financing: The Unsecured Leveraged Buyout

Leonard Caronia

Psssst, would you like to buy a company? You need very little money. With 1 or 2 percent of the purchase price you might acquire more than 50 percent ownership. Interested? Just be prepared to put your career, security, and a little capital at risk, and you may be on the road to riches. And don't think that the only companies available are those which have been left for dead. In fact, the best leveraged buyout candidates are the most consistently profitable businesses. Unfortunately, these high-quality companies rarely sell at prices below book value, so financing based on asset values may not be sufficient. But don't despair. There are dozens of lenders and equity investors eager to assist you by providing financing well in excess of asset values. Better yet, the total financing will be unsecured!

Before you conclude that these lenders and investors represent the epitome of naivete or, perhaps, the brute financier that conducts business in a city's back alleys, let me assure you that they include the largest and most sophisticated financial institutions in the world. Their investment decisions are based on the company's projected capability to generate cash flow, which can be used to service debt and generate shareholder wealth.

In an unsecured LBO the acquisition is financed through the sale of debt and equity securities to a group of lender/investor participants. Unlike an asset-based leveraged buyout, where the structure and amount of financing is closely related to the estimated liquidation value of the underlying assets, unsecured investors rely almost entirely on the company's projected cash flow. Unsecured leveraged acquisition financings are often referred to as cash flow leveraged buyouts.

In a cash flow leveraged buyout, investors take a long-term view of the business, which is usually based on the company's past history of stable profitability. These long-term investors will typically provide financing with a 10- to 15-year maturity, and at a fixed interest rate. This financing structure offers tremendous advantages to a highly leveraged company. The long maturity permits a gradual debt repayment schedule which can be matched against projected cash flow. It minimizes debt servicing requirements in the early years which might force a refinancing at an inauspicious time. To the extent interest rates are fixed, one eliminates the potentially disastrous consequences of increasing interest rates on an acquisition financed almost exclusively with debt.

As you might expect, these real advantages of a cash flow leveraged buyout are not free—or even inexpensive. Lenders and investors recognize that they take a substantial equity risk with a highly leveraged, long-term unsecured financing. Therefore they generally insist on sharing in the company's expected future success by participating in the equity ownership of the company. This ownership sharing is usually referred to as an equity kicker. The equity kicker can be as little as 10 percent of the company's shares or as much as 80 percent. The actual amount of the equity kicker is based on the perceived risk of the financing, the amount of equity needed to obtain a desired return on investment, and of course, competition among investors. The determination of the appropriate size of the equity kicker is discussed later in this chapter.

One additional advantage of a cash flow buyout is that it enables the buyer to finance a purchase price well in excess of the company's book value or real asset value. The only limit on the amount of available financing is the firm's expected ability to service debt and provide an adequate equity return. This financing power is particularly important when higher corporate earnings drive up acquisition prices. Remember, the prospective leveraged buyout bidder must often compete against well-monied corporate buyers on larger target candidates. The cash flow structure in many cases allows the LBO buyer to bid competitively, regardless of asset values, unless the corporate buyer is willing to pay an additional premium due to perceived strategic synergy.

The debt financing in a cash flow leveraged buyout is usually left unsecured. This is done for two reasons. First, long-term lenders and equity investors are not basing their financing decision on asset values, so there is little value in closely monitoring specific assets over time. Most cash flow LBO investors have neither the staff nor the skill necessary to manage an asset-based loan. Second, since security is not critical to the investors, leaving the assets of a highly leveraged company unencumbered occasionally enhances the firm's ability to obtain favorable terms on trade credit.

However, don't believe that these sophisticated investors have left themselves unprotected. A mandatory provision in the legal documentation will specify that security can not be given to any other creditor, and if by some chance it is, the LBO lender would have the right to become equally secured. This provision is termed the "negative pledge" clause.

In summary, the unsecured cash flow leveraged buyout can provide financing well in excess of the underlying asset value, allow a long-term debt repayment schedule, offer a fixed interest rate, and enhance the firm's ability to obtain favorable trade credit terms. Furthermore, the long-term, fixed interest rate debt can significantly reduce the risk of a leveraged acquisition. This advantage is discussed later in this chapter.

CHARACTERISTICS OF A SUCCESSFUL UNSECURED LEVERAGED BUYOUT

When discussing leveraged buyouts, one often attempts to outline the criteria which distinguish a potentially successful transaction. The risk of such definition is that it tends to be either so specific that most completed financings represent exceptions or so general that it becomes difficult to envision a company that might not qualify. The skill and experience of a leveraged buyout financial adviser or a sophisticated investor is usually necessary to determine the feasibility of a cash flow leveraged buyout. Therefore consider these characteristics as only a general indication of what lenders and investors look for in a cash flow leveraged buyout. The three principal considerations are: (1) projected cash flow, (2) management, and (3) a value-added factor.

Projected Cash Flow

The ability to confidently project adequate cash flow is absolutely essential. Therefore, investors look closely at the consistency of historical earnings and the stability of profit margins. Some revenue and earnings growth will usually be necessary to maintain a competitive position and to provide the equity investors with a satisfactory return. The company's internally generated cash flow must be able to service the increased working capital requirements, capital expenditures, and (if applicable) research and development costs. Additional considerations which influence projected cash flow include: (1) the ability to pass price increases on to customers; (2) the firm's market share (a larger market share tends to minimize the impact of economic declines and predatory pricing by competitors); (3) production costs compared to competitors'; (4) the diversification of product lines and the importance of the end uses for the products; and (5) the loyalty of and/or dependency on existing customers and suppliers.

If surplus assets are expected to be sold, the ability of the buyout company to service its debt must not rely on the anticipated timing or proceeds of such sales.

Management

The importance of management in a leveraged buyout can not be overemphasized. Investors recognize that no matter how closely they analyze a transaction, adverse events will occur which were not contemplated. As they occur, the investor's success is almost entirely dependent on the skill, judgment, and actions of management. It is for this reason that investors eagerly agree to management's ownership of a substantial part of the company for what is usually a very small percentage of the purchase price. In general, investors look for management's ability and commitment, as well as satisfactory internal financial controls and management information systems.

The Value-Added Factor

The value-added factor is a sometimes elusive concept, but one that is present in almost every unsecured cash flow leveraged buyout. If a leveraged buyout management merely allows the firm to operate in the future as it had in the past, then any premium return on equity is solely the result of the increased debt. A leveraged buyout structured on this basis can be successful, but the increased risk leaves little room for error.

The value-added factor, which is commonly referred to as "the story," is instrumental because it allows the company to pay off debt more quickly, reduce the risk of the investment, and perhaps most importantly, increase the investment return to the equity investors. These factors can be either a tangible or an intangible item that enables the buyer to elevate the company to a higher level of profitability and cash flow within a short time after the acquisition. Value-added factors can take many forms, but the ones listed below are most frequently observed.

Emphasis on the generation of cash flow instead of taxable income and increased earnings per share by management.

Elimination of excessive parent company management fees or excessive owner salaries or benefits.

Sale of excess low-earning assets to raise cash that can be used for debt reduction.

Freeing management from restrictions imposed by parent company direction and controls.

Opportunity to penetrate new markets that prior owners ignored.

Inefficient operations that can be improved by new owners.

In general, the more tangible the value-added factor, the easier it will be to convince lenders and investors to finance the buyout transaction. A buyout group should construct a comprehensive and documented business plan that stresses "the story" and builds a strong case for significant cash flow increases. It should be recognized that intangible factors are much less convincing than tangible, quantifiable plans. For example, it is difficult to quantify the added value that arises from increasing management freedom. However, intangible value-added factors can be very attractive to an investor group when combined with the measurable economic and financial factors necessary for a successful leveraged buyout.

CAPITAL STRUCTURE

A cash flow leveraged buyout provides a unique opportunity—the ability to create a desired balance sheet capital structure. Nearly the entire liability side of the new company's balance sheet can be tailored to match the projected cash flows and the equity investor's tolerance for financial risk. The only constraint is that the financing plan must be acceptable to lenders and equity investors. As shown in Table 6–1, the permutations of capital structuring are almost endless. This section discusses a rationale to construct a capital structure, but professional advice in this critical area is almost certainly worth its cost. A poor capital structure can destroy an otherwise satisfactory leveraged acquisition.

Although the liability structure of the buyout company goes through a complete metamorphosis at the time of acquisition, the assets and earning power of the firm remain unchanged. For the buyout investment to be successful, the company must be able to sustain its preinterest expense earnings in order to reestablish the unleveraged balance sheet that existed prior to the buyout. In the initial years, cash flow is used to build an adequate liquidity cushion and then is increas-

TABLE 6–1   Buyout Capital Structure

Securities	Percent of capitalization	Primary lender/investor
Short or intermediate-term senior debt (payout 2–6 years).	5–20%	Commercial banks.
Long-term senior and subordinated debt (payout 5–15 years).	40–80	Life insurance companies, some banks, LBO funds.
Preferred stock (payout 5–20 years).	10–20	Life insurance and venture capital companies.
Common stock.	1–20 / 100%	Life insurance companies, venture capital companies, investment bankers management.

ingly applied to the reduction of debt. Typically, short- or intermediate-term bank debt is repaid first.

After approximately four years, the rate at which funded debt is retired with retained earnings accelerates, and the buyout company should emerge from its initial period of high risk. This reduction in risk is evidenced by a return to a capital structure typical of a firm in its particular industry. The construction of a capital structure should incorporate appropriate trade-offs among several competing factors. These factors include: (1) the cost of the financing, (2) the company's ability to sustain risk associated with floating rate debt, (3) the predictability of cash flow generation, and (4) management's tolerance for risk.

In Table 6–1, for example, each security listed tends to be more expensive than those listed above it. For instance, long-term senior debt is typically more expensive than short-term debt but less expensive than preferred stock. Therefore, if a buyer wanted the lowest cost financing, the choice would be 100 percent floating-rate bank financing with a maturity of about four years. While in theory this might be the least expensive, the new company would be incurring substantial risks. A substantial increase in interest rates would likely be disastrous, although risk minimization devices (such as cash caps and hedges, which will be discussed later in this chapter) are being used with increasing frequency. The company also would be forced to refinance in the fourth year, which could become a very unpleasant experience if earnings are weak, the economic outlook is poor, credit availability is limited, leveraged buyouts fall out of favor, or for any almost innumerable other reasons.

In this example, the buying group has bet its future on interest rates and the capital market. These risks cannot be managed or even influenced. Unfortunately, the competitive financial market will not protect the buyer from arranging this risky capital structure. Too many eager banks have provided just such short-term, floating-rate acquisition financing.

The opposite extreme, while more conservative, is equally inappropriate. A capitalization could be structured with a large amount of equity and a lesser amount of long-term, fixed-rate senior debt. This would be a very safe capitalization for the buyer, but it would provide such a poor return on investment for the management group that there would be little likelihood of any meaningful reward in computing a risk : reward formula.

Attaining an appropriate balance between risk and cost is necessary, but the best solution is anything but obvious. A detailed set of operating projections must be prepared and extensive sensitivity analysis performed to measure the impact of changes in revenues, margins, and interest rates. The conclusions must then be packaged into a capital structure acceptable to investors. It is detailed, time-consuming work; but if properly done, the result is a long-term workable capitalization at the lowest possible cost.

THE PARTICIPANTS

Participants in an unsecured leveraged buyout effort, like those in an acrobatic stunt, rely on each other for support and balance. Each member has an individual responsibility which, if not executed properly, will result in the likelihood of casualties. The results of a failed leveraged buyout are severe indeed. They often include unemployment and a large loss of money. The risk of an LBO failure can be minimized with a proper capital structure and by each participant properly performing its assigned role.

A successful leveraged buyout usually requires the participation of management, lenders, equity investors, lawyers, accountants, and a financial adviser. Although thousands of each are readily available, the very specific requirements of an unsecured leveraged buyout demand careful selection of the leveraged buyout team.

Management

In addition to the necessary management capabilities discussed earlier in this chapter, management also must be both financially astute and psychologically able to handle a large amount of debt. Management must recognize that the incurrence of a heavy debt package will change "business as usual." The significant debt service requirements in a cash flow leveraged buyout add tremendous importance to cash flow forecasting, profit center management, pricing decisions, and competitors' actions. The management of a highly leveraged company must quickly and appropriately respond to changing conditions, since its ability to withstand adversity is much more limited than that of a more conservatively capitalized firm.

The quality of management is the most important determinant of the success of an unsecured cash flow leveraged buyout. Key managers almost always participate in the ownership of the new company. Although their ownership share is sometimes small compared to investors that provide most of the capital, management can profit handsomely if the buyout is successful. Also, it is not unusual for the management group to use the company's cash flow to eventually repurchase the ownership shares from the investor group.

Lenders

Lenders in cash flow leveraged buyouts typically include banks, insurance companies, LBO funds, and (to a limited extent) pension funds. Historically, the banks provided short-term, floating-rate financing to meet working capital requirements, while insurance companies, LBO funds, and pension funds provided more permanent financing in the form of long-term, fixed-rate debt. More recently some banks have moved to exclude insurance companies from some buyouts by offering financing with maturities as long as 10 years and protection from rising interest rates through a variety of creative mechanisms. These mechanisms include interest rate swaps (a contract with a bank to exchange a floating interest rate for a fixed rate); "bow tie" arrangements where interest expense above a specified rate is added to the principal of the loan (also referred to as "cash caps"); and purchased rate protection where, for a fee, a bank will undertake the risk of interest rates rising above a specified level.

In the past, when banks opted for shorter maturities and floating interest rates, they rarely received any equity kicker. Today, those banks providing longer-term debt are much more likely to request both equity and front-end fees.

Insurance companies still tend to provide the most favorable terms for the long-term debt capital required for cash flow leveraged buyouts. Ten- to 15-year maturities with no required principal payments for at least 3 years is common. Fixed interest rates are still readily available. On the other hand, an equity kicker (usually in the form of common stock warrants) is almost a certainty. The size of the equity kicker is based on the lender's yield objective and the acquired company's cash flow projections. Calculating the equity kicker is discussed in greater detail later in this chapter.

When selecting a lender-participant for a cash flow leveraged buyout, there is no substitute for experience. A lender is very much a long-term partner in a buyout, and this partner will typically have extensive operating and financial covenants with which to exercise its authority. No matter how well planned a buyout may be, unexpected events and opportunities will occur. When they do, an experienced buyout lender may be less likely to overreact. Without question, the best leveraged buyout lender may not be the one offering the lowest cost. Experience and reputation are the best measures of good lender participants.

Equity Investors

The principal source of equity money for unsecured leveraged buyouts is the venture capital company. The venture capitalist provides the highest-risk institutional capital and, as a result, requires the highest return. Venture capital investments are typically in the form of subordinated debt or preferred stock. The investments always include a significant share of the equity ownership, either through a direct purchase of common stock or by way of warrants. A venture capitalist generally requires an annual return of better than 35 percent on its investment. This return represents both current income from the subordinated debentures or preferred stock and capital gains on its share of the equity ownership.

As with lender-participants, the best equity investors are experienced in leveraged buyouts. Venture capitalists often require representation on the board of directors. Therefore, a good venture capital participant should have knowledge of the company's business and be able to work cohesively with management.

Lawyers and Accountants

The assistance of experienced lawyers and accountants before the buyout is completed is necessary to avoid as many unpleasant surprises as possible. Buyers who try to avoid these fees or who hire counsel without buyout experience are sometimes shocked to uncover unfunded pension liabilities or income tax recapture expenses. Good tax and legal advice is readily available, and lenders, equity investors, and management should insist on it.

Financial Advisers/Investment Bankers

There may not be a better example than an unsecured leveraged buyout to demonstrate the need and benefit of a skilled financial adviser. As discussed above, a successful cash flow buyout requires the cooperative effort of many different participants, each with different interests, expectations, return requirements, and—for the experienced participants—a limited amount of time available to spend prospecting or structuring new deals.

Someone must identify the investors who will have an interest in a particular buyout. The financing must be structured to be acceptable to each and every lender and equity investor, and appropriate expected returns must be demonstrated. The buyout must be properly presented to the investors to spark initial interest and support the critical projections. Potential problems must be identified as early as possible and reviewed by tax or legal counsel.

In addition, competition among lenders and equity investors may be necessary in order to obtain the best financing. Someone must coordinate responses and constantly restructure each investor's participation to minimize the cost while maintaining an appropriate capitalization. Whether or not a financial adviser is hired, the above tasks must be appropriately executed. Mistakes will be expensive, or very possibly fatal, to the leveraged buyout.

A financial adviser experienced in leveraged buyouts will have much more than a working knowledge of each of the prospective participant's desires, requirements, and capabilities. The adviser can be used to select the best participants, analyze the trade-off between cost minimization and capital structure risk, provide lenders and investors with the information they need to analyze and obtain investment approval, and coordinate the entire transaction so that surprises are minimized and participants (including the seller) maintain interest in completing the buyout.

The role of a financial adviser should not be confused with that of a broker. A broker may identify and bring together a buyer and seller, but that is a long way from structuring and completing a complex unsecured cash flow leveraged buyout. A financial adviser is usually hired by the management group of the new company. The fee is typically about 1 percent of the purchase price. Occasionally, the financial adviser is paid with stock of the new company and may even choose to be one of the equity investors.

Other Participants

In certain circumstances, other participants can be included in an unsecured leveraged buyout. Their inclusion is usually made necessary by a specific risk, opportunity, or shortcoming in a prospective transaction. These participants can include employees through an employee stock ownership plan (ESOP), seller financing, small business investment companies (SBICs), key customers of the company, and wealthy individuals or families from either the United States or other countries interested in investment opportunities.

ELIMINATING THE MYSTERY OF THE EQUITY KICKER

Managers of prospective leveraged buyouts are usually surprised when they are informed of the equity kicker. Sometimes (but rarely) the surprise is pleasant. Most of the time, the surprise is met with a reaction approaching shock. The equity kicker is so important to the cost and the success of the financing that any surprise should be eliminated. Management and the investors should mutually understand how the equity kicker was determined.

The following example calculates an equity kicker on the long-term debt of an unsecured leveraged buyout. The calculation of a venture capitalist's equity kicker would be similar.

1. Projections. The operating projections are the keystone to determining the size of the equity kicker. The income projection table projects sales to increase at 10 percent and net income (before any adjustment for interest expense) to remain at 5 percent of sales.

Income Projection ($ Millions)					
Year	1	2	3	4	5
Sales	$100.0	$110.0	$121.0	$133.0	$146.0
Net income before interest expense	5.0	5.5	6.1	6.7	7.3

2. Purchase Price. $50 million, which represents 10 times the first year's net income before interest expense.

3. Capitalization of the New Company.

	Millions of dollars	Percent of capitalization
Bank debt—5-year revolving credit at prime + 1 percent	$ 5.0	10.0%
Long-term debt—15 years at 13 percent	40.0	80.0
Equity investors and management	5.0	10.0
	$50.0	100.0

4. Long-Term Lender's Return Requirements.

The new company is capitalized with 90 percent debt and 10 percent equity. A more normal capitalization would be 50 percent debt and 50 percent equity. A 50 percent debt:equity ratio would have $25 million of debt and $25 million of equity. Therefore, $20 million of the actual long-term debt ($25 million − $5 million of actual equity) really has an equity risk which requires an equity return. This $20 million of debt is called "equity-equivalent debt."

The typical required annual return on equity-equivalent debt ranges between 20 percent and 35 percent. In this example, we will assume that the lender expects 25 percent per year. Therefore, as shown below, the long-term lender has a 12 percent annual shortfall which must be obtained from the equity kicker.

		Required Return		
	(1) Amount of debt ($ millions)	(2) Expected return	(3) Coupon (current return)	(4) Annual return shortfall (2 − 3)
Debt	$20.0	13%	13%	0%
Equity-equivalent debt	20.0	25	13	12
Total long-term debt	$40.0			

A 12 percent annual shortfall on $20 million is equal to $2.4 million per year. A long-term lender usually projects to recapture this forgone income at the fifth year of the investment. Each year then, for five years, this $2.4 million shortfall can be considered to be reinvested in the company and must also earn at a 25 percent compounded rate. The future value of an annual $2.4 million shortfall in five years, compounded at 25 percent, is $19.7 million. In other words, at the end of the fifth year, the long-term lender will project a $19.7 million payment in lieu of the $2.4 million dollar annual shortfall.

5. Value of the Company.

If the company earns $7.3 million (before interest expense) in the fifth year and sells for 10 times earnings, the value of the firm would be $73 million. However, the value of the equity is equal to the value of the firm *less* the amount of outstanding debt. If we assume that $10 million of the debt has been repaid over five years, the projected value of the equity at the end of the fifth year is $33 million ($73 million less $40 million of outstanding debt).

6. Equity Kicker Required. The long-term lender's shortfall is $19.7 million at the end of the fifth year. An equity value of $33.0 million is projected when this payment is expected. Therefore, the long-term lender would require an equity kicker, probably in the form of common stock warrants, amounting to approximately 60 percent of the company ($19.7 million divided by $33.0 million).

Obviously, the value of the firm in the fifth year can be very different from that projected by the long-term lender. However, that projection will be the basis for determining the equity kicker. Some lenders and investors will agree to an adjustable equity kicker which is based on actual earnings in future years. This is appropriate when projected operations are significantly different from historical performance.

OTHER OBSERVATIONS

Importance of Projections

In the above example, if the long-term lender could have been convinced that sales would increase 15 percent per annum instead of 10 percent, the required equity kicker would be reduced from 60 percent to 41 percent. This 19 percent additional ownership share would belong to management. It should be no surprise that a great amount of time is spent discussing new market opportunities, potential cost savings, projected inflation rates, and other value-added factors that favorably impact projected earnings. Management is well counseled to consider projections very seriously, as well as to attempt to quantify and verify any variations from historical performance. A surprisingly common attitude by management groups that projections are worthless guesses about an uncertain future can be very costly indeed.

Exit Strategies

An important consideration of any lender or investor receiving an equity kicker is both how and when the equity return can be realized. This concern is commonly referred to as an exit strategy. Generally, a lender or equity investor desires to realize its equity return within five to seven years of the investment. The equity profit can be earned if the company is sold, if public shares are successfully offered, or if the management group repurchases the shares from the lenders and investors. Occasionally, the financing is structured to allow either the investors or management to force the other to repurchase its shares. Obviously, the terms and prices for these put-and-call options are the source of substantial negotiations. Competent advisers are suggested for the uninitiated.

Other Forms of Equity Kickers

Equity kickers also can be in the form of contingent payments, which are based on sales or earnings of the company. Contingent payments are preferred by investors when an exit strategy can not be identified, but are generally less attractive than ownership equity kickers.

CONCLUDING COMMENT

The economic downturn in the early 1980s resulted in many companies being sold at prices near or even below book value. This situation created unusually attractive opportunities for leveraged buyout entrepreneurs since asset-based financing was readily available.

Unfortunately for buyers, the recent economic expansion and optimism have dramatically increased selling prices. As acquisition prices rose significantly above liquidation and book values, it became increasingly difficult to achieve a high degree of financial leverage with secured asset-based financing. Unsecured leveraged buyouts are based on projected cash flows and do not require loans to be supported by asset values. Therefore, today's higher purchase prices still can be financed through a leveraged acquisition if cash flow is adequate.

The good news associated with rising purchase prices is that more and more attractive businesses are being offered for sale. Many public companies are placing increased attention on their basic businesses and selling profitable operations that do not strategically fit. Executives with good business experience and judgment possess a valuable asset that still can be used to gain the financial support of lenders and equity investors interested in financing leveraged buyouts. An unsecured leveraged buyout provides managers with a rare opportunity to capitalize fully on their experience and own a significant equity interest in their own firm, often for a relatively nominal investment.

Many articles recently have been written espousing the risks and disadvantages of leveraged buyouts. However, newly wealthy management groups and many happy investors provide testimony to the historical success of well-constructed leveraged buyouts. Good investment sense may be becoming too rare a commodity, and some ill-prepared investors will make mistakes and lose money. But well-conceived and properly capitalized leveraged buyouts remain as attractive and sensible as they have been in the past. A leveraged buyout continues to be a road to ownership and riches for some managers.

Chapter 7

Seeking Financing: The Role of the Venture Capitalist

John A. Canning, Jr.

In spite of the heavy, sometimes negative publicity leveraged buyouts have achieved recently, the fact is that LBO financing does have its place in the economic world. While it is true that prices have tended to escalate and that both buyers who overpay and lenders who overfinance may suffer, the experienced players who are patient and adhere to proven disciplines in analyzing and structuring buyouts will be not only survivors but winners. A leveraged buyout, if properly structured, is a sound method of financing the transfer of ownership of an ongoing business that can provide each financing tier of a buyout with a return commensurate with the risk taken.

There is no magic to a leveraged buyout. It does not create value where none exists. It is an appropriate financing technique for the acquisition of only those businesses which fit a certain profile. There are many elements to be considered in determining whether a business has such a profile, including its financial and operating characteristics, its management, the purchase price to be paid, and the financing structure. Once the target has been identified, however, one of the most important decisions a prospective buyer must make is selecting the right financing partners.

As indicated elsewhere in this book, there are several different sources of debt and equity financing, with each varying investment criteria and risk:reward profiles. There are circumstances under

which a business can be safely acquired using debt financing exclusively. In today's competitive environment some leveraged buyouts are
being financed almost exclusively with debt, with buyers retaining
most of the equity while putting little capital at risk. This is, however,
the exception and not the rule. More often a buyer will find that he
cannot obtain sufficient debt financing for a leveraged acquisition
without an adequate equity base.

Even if lenders do not require the injection of new equity, a buyer
must carefully consider the trade-offs of retaining more equity against
surrendering equity in order to give the acquired business a stronger
balance sheet. He must weigh the risk : reward parameters of the business and its likelihood of succeeding without the additional equity.
Generally, experienced lenders and entrepreneurs alike require adequate equity financing to provide sufficient operating room in the
event of unplanned contingencies. Choosing a financing structure
which "bets the ranch" to retain equity ownership can have a punitive
effect if things don't go as planned.

WHEN TO CONSIDER VENTURE FINANCING

Venture capitalists have proven to be a significant source for equity
financings in leveraged buyouts. This chapter focuses on the role of
venture capitalists in financing leveraged buyouts. Another significant
source of equity for leveraged buyout financing not dealt with here is
leveraged buyout specialists such as Kohlberg, Kravis, Roberts & Co.;
Forstmann, Little & Co.; AEA Investors, Inc.; and Gibbons, Green, van
Amerongen, Ltd., to name a few. These groups generally control large
pools of funds provided by institutional investors which they can commit to purchase equity in leveraged buyouts. Unlike venture capitalists, they invest only in leveraged buyouts, are usually interested only
in companies with purchase prices in excess of $50 million, and almost
always gain economic and voting control of the acquired company.

Most venture capitalists, on the other hand, are engaged in a wide
range of high-risk investing, often involving companies in start-up
modes or very early stages of development. Leveraged buyout financing is usually their lowest-risk business. Most venture capitalists experienced in financing buyouts will consider financing acquisitions
with purchase prices of as low as $5 million and will participate with-
out taking economic or voting control if the economics justify.

In determining whether venture equity financing is appropriate, it is
important to understand what besides money venture capitalists bring
to the table, their investment objectives, what kinds of businesses they
will finance, and what role they expect to play after the financing
closes.

VALUE ADDED BY VENTURE CAPITALISTS

The need for high-risk equity capital is usually the first reason a prospective buyer seeks venture financing. Yet the prospective buyer should look to a venture investor to provide more than money.

Credibility with Seller

One of the most difficult tasks facing a prospective buyer is getting the seller to take him seriously. Often a prospective buyer cannot get access to financial and related information necessary to make a purchase decision or to structure an offer until he can clearly demonstrate his ability to finance the purchase. Unless the buyer is existing management or has significant financial resources, this can be an insurmountable obstacle. Sellers are less reluctant to provide the needed information to an experienced venture capitalist with a demonstrated capability for financing leveraged buyouts. An early alliance with a venture partner may get the deal in the door.

Assistance in Financing Arrangements and Negotiations

Often a prospective buyer is faced with several tasks which must be completed in a short time frame. In addition to exercising his own due diligence and coordinating the legal and accounting review necessary to determine whether to make an offer to purchase the target company, he must arrange for the financing of the purchase and structure an offer to the seller. A buyer who has selected a venture capitalist as an equity partner should expect him to assist in performing these functions. Venture capitalists experienced in financing leveraged buyouts can usually call on lawyers and accountants who are experts in investigating, documenting, and negotiating leveraged buyouts and optimizing available tax benefits in structuring the purchase.

The venture capitalist will bring in other equity investors if needed, and can save the buyer invaluable time by identifying the sources of debt financing most appropriate for the proposed transaction. The buyer often is able to get access to debt financing which becomes available because the lender has had prior financing relationships with the venture capitalist. In addition, the venture capitalist usually has his thumb on the pulse of the market and is aware of the best financing terms currently available. As an equity participant, he has the same incentive as the buyer to select the financing source and negotiate terms which will provide the maximum return on investment.

The prospective buyer should also take advantage of the venture capitalist's experience in negotiating and structuring leveraged buyout purchase contracts. The venture capitalist's participation in negotiations with the seller should provide added assurances that the necessary representations, warranties, indemnifications, and postclosing adjustments are in place to ensure that the buyers receive what they pay for.

The venture capitalist's active involvement may also help to neutralize any bargaining advantage the seller may enjoy in situations where the prospective buyer is employed by the seller or because of the prospective buyer's natural enthusiasm to close the transaction.

Cross-Utilization of Talent

Experienced venture capitalists usually have a reservoir of high-quality management talent from previous buyouts they've financed. It is common for venture firms to enlist these managers as board members of, or advisers to, new buyouts if they have special experience or talents that are appropriate. This can be a valuable resource, not otherwise readily available, to the buyer of a new business who has not had the experience of operating with a highly leveraged balance sheet.

VENTURE CAPITALISTS' INVESTMENT OBJECTIVES

Before deciding on venture financing for a leveraged buyout, a prospective buyer should understand the returns venture capitalists expect, the financial risk they expect the buyer to take, the anticipated timing and method of liquidating the investment, and other rights venture capitalists typically receive.

What Returns Do Venture Investors Expect?

It is the natural goal of every prospective acquirer of a business to look for a financing method which will permit him to close the transaction and relinquish as little of the equity as possible to the other financing participants. Experienced venture capitalists who specialize in leveraged buyouts generally provide the highest-risk financing tier in a leveraged buyout—the equity layer necessary to obtain the required debt financing. They expect to receive a sufficient equity interest to compensate them for the financial risk they are taking. Their targeted compound annual rates of return are rarely less than 35 percent and often exceed 50 percent.

Venture capitalists are uniform in two respects. First, they expect to realize the major portion of their anticipated return through appreciation of the equity of the company financed. While they may take part of their return in the form of dividend or interest payments, they will always require an equity participation. Second, they will not agree to a fixed rate of return or a cap on their upside potential. For example, if a venture capitalist targets a 40 percent compound annual rate of return, he will not grant the right to repurchase his investment at a price which yields that return. The reason is simple. To achieve an overall return on 40 percent from all buyouts the venture capitalist finances, he must exceed that level enough times to offset the investments which fall short of his target.

How much of the common equity will a venture capitalist require to provide leveraged buyout financing? It has been said that it is easier to determine how many peanuts an elephant can eat. However, there is some rationality to the venture capitalist's decision process. Usually there is no preset amount of equity a venture capitalist requires. Rather, it is purely an economic decision. To determine the percent of the company he must own to achieve his targeted return, the venture capitalist forecasts how much the company will be worth at the time he expects to liquidate his investment. The following example illustrates how this process might work.

Management of Company X has reached an agreement with X's parent company to purchase X for $20 million in cash. The purchase price represents a multiple of five times X's previous year's pretax, preinterest income of $4 million. A bank has agreed to provide term loan financing of $16 million if $4 million in equity is raised. Management is willing to invest $500,000 in equity and approaches a venture capitalist for the remaining $3.5 million of equity required.

After reviewing X's businesses and management's five-year projections, the venture capitalist concludes that even under a pessimistic interest rate and economic scenario:

1. Company X's pretax, preinterest income for the fifth year following the purchase should be at least $6 million.
2. Company X should generate sufficient cash flow to repay $12 million of the $16 million acquisition debt by the end of the fifth year.
3. Company X could be resold after five years for $30 million, or five times its fifth-year pretax, preinterest income (the same multiple for which it was purchased).

Accordingly, if Company X were sold for $30 million after five years, the equity holders would receive $26 million after the remaining $4 million of acquisition debt is repaid.

The venture capitalist offers to provide the needed $3.5 million in equity in the form of a cumulative redeemable preferred stock with a

---

TABLE 7–1   Company X's Buyout: Effects of Financing
(\$ Thousands)

	Total equity dollars invested	Percent of equity dollars invested	Percent of common received	Annual dividend	Dollar split of sale proceeds	Compound annual rate of return (includes dividends)
Venture capitalist	\$3,500	87.5%	60%	\$350	\$15,600	41%
Management	500	12.5	40	—	10,400	83
Total	\$4,000	100.0	100	\$350	\$26,000	50

---

10 percent annual dividend rate and for the right to convert \$750,000 of the preferred into 60 percent of Company X's common stock. Management's \$500,000 would buy 40 percent of X's common stock. With this offer, the venture capitalist is trying to achieve three investment goals:

1. Invest his money in a senior position to management's investment.
2. Receive a preferential return in the form of current income.
3. Achieve an overall compound annual rate of return in excess of 40 percent.

Table 7–1 illustrates the comparative economic effect of this financing, assuming the equity holders receive \$26 million from a sale after five years. Here management invests 12.5 percent of the equity dollars and receives 40 percent of the common stock. The venture capitalist provides 87.5 percent of the equity dollars and receives 60 percent of the common. The venture capitalist is willing to accept less than its proportionate share of the common stock in exchange for its senior position and the dividend income and to provide added economic incentive to management. As the table indicates, the returns can be very attractive for both management and the venture investor.

What Financial Risk Must Owner-Managers Take?

Venture capitalists are uniform in their requirement that the active management of a business acquired in a leveraged buyout must have an equity stake in the company. In fact, most venture capitalists refer to leveraged buyouts as management buyouts. They will not finance leveraged buyouts unless the key managers are equity owners and have invested their own money in the company. As equity owners, the managers have an economic incentive to run the business with a view to maximizing return on investment. Their success naturally inures to the benefit of the venture investors.

The investment of their own money is the key managers' affirmation of their belief in the company's prospects. The amount invested, in absolute terms, is not important as long as each key manager has invested a meaningful portion of his assets. Most venture capitalists don't expect a manager to mortgage his house or risk his children's education. The amount invested is designed to motivate the manager to devote his full attention to operating the business without the threat of financial ruin if the business falters.

The venture capitalist tries to strike a balance to achieve upside motivation and downside protection. The managers must have a large enough equity stake to provide the prospects of a significant reward for a successful effort, and place sufficient assets at risk to ensure they cannot comfortably walk away from the business if things get tough. Experience has taught venture capitalists important lessons about investing along with management in leveraged buyouts.

Key managers of a division of a large corporation to be acquired in a leveraged buyout are usually offered the opportunity to invest in the new company. In some cases they do not view this as opportunity but rather as a requirement to keep their jobs. As a result, the investment is not an affirmation of the business's prospects, but an investment made under the perceived threat of a loss of employment. Accordingly, great care should be taken to ensure that key managers are willingly investing their funds because of the upside potential they perceive.

Also it is common for managers to warmly embrace the concept of a leveraged buyout. They tend to be optimistic and are motivated by the opportunity to become equity participants in a business previously owned by others. Yet a leveraged buyout, by its nature, increases the financial risk of the business. These managers often have worked in the secure environment of a large corporation. Managers who are investing a meaningful portion of their assets must be carefully advised of the increased risks inherent in a buyout before they make their investment decision.

One situation venture capitalists tend to avoid is the leveraged acquisition of a business from owners who are key managers, unless the owners are willing to reinvest the aftertax proceeds realized in the sale. If key managers cash out in a prior sale and do not reinvest the sale proceeds, most venture capitalists fear that these managers will not have the appropriate economic motivation to achieve the desired upside potential or downside protection.

Liquidation Expectations

Venture capitalists are not permanent partners. They generally invest with a view to liquidating their investment in a five- to seven-year time frame. Before choosing a venture capitalist as a financing partner, an entrepreneur should reach a clear understanding with the venture capitalist regarding the timing and method of liquidating the latter's investment.

Venture capitalists prefer to finance entrepreneurs who are motivated by the desire to maximize capital and who have a similar time horizon for maximizing return on investment. They will shy away from providing financing to an entrepreneur who would be reluctant to sell his business to the highest bidder—one motivated more by ego than by capital accumulation.

Since leveraged buyout companies are generally engaged in lower-growth, mundane business, the public markets do not provide a reliable liquidation mechanism. While venture capitalists will generally have the contractual right to require the company to register its equity securities for public sale, the anticipated method of exiting the investment is usually the sale of the entire company to a third party. If the venture capitalists have majority control, they may be able to force such a sale. As a practical matter, a third-party sale is not feasible without the agreement and cooperation of the key management of the company. Usually a company with an unhappy management team, or with a team that will leave after the sale, has little value to a prospective third-party purchaser.

If the owner-managers are not inclined to see the business sold in five to seven years and to stay on as managers if requested by the purchaser, venture financing is not appropriate. Even if the business is successful, the prospects of not realizing the expected return would make the proposition unattractive to a venture investor.

In situations where the venture investors have a minority interest in the business, they customarily provide for the right to "put" their investment to the company or the majority owners after a specified time period (usually at least five years). This is a common mechanism venture capitalists use to protect themselves from being forced to remain in an illiquid minority equity investment.

The price at which a put is exercisable can vary. Often it is a fixed price designed to give the venture investor an acceptable return. It can also be pegged to the company's book value at the time of exercise or to a multiple of the most recent year's earnings or cash flow. Because these measures can vary with down years and may not reflect the true value of the company, the put is often exercisable at the company's "fair market value" at the time of exercise. A contractual mechanism which includes the appointment of an impartial arbitrator is usually established for determining fair market value.

A put is not intended to be a satisfactory method to liquidate an investment. Rather it is a protective device which is intended to force the majority owners to provide an exit mechanism for the minority venture investors. It is usually exercised only when the company has been successful and the owner-managers and the venture investors disagree over the timing and method of maximizing their return on investment. It is designed to bring the majority owners to the bargaining table to agree on the value of the venture investor's equity interest and to find another investor or lender to finance the acquisition of that interest.

A put is a moot right when the company has performed poorly. Its exercise is usually prohibited by existing financing agreements; even if permitted, financing for the put is usually nonexistent.

When faced with the request for a put, owner-managers usually request the right to call the venture investors' equity. This is a reasonable request, but one that is rarely granted by venture investors. Most venture investors will not limit their potential upside. Regardless of the measure (e.g., a multiple of earnings) selected to determine the call value of the venture investors' equity, it can usually be affected by management of the company. In addition, the call places the timing and method of liquidation in the hands of the owner-managers. An exercise following a down year may result in a price that doesn't accurately reflect the true value or future prospects of the company.

Restrictions on Owner-Managers' Liquidity

Since the venture investor is usually placing his bet on management's commitment to make a success of the business, owner-managers can expect a venture investor to restrict their ability to sell shares in the company prior to the time the venture investor sells. Some of the restrictions commonly used are:

Right of first refusal, which gives the company or the venture investors the right to buy the owner-managers' shares prior to a sale to a third party. Customarily the purchase price is tied to the original purchase price or the company's book value and is designed to penalize a sale (except upon death or disability) which occurs prior to the expected maturity of the venture investors' investment.

Take-along agreement, which prohibits the owner-managers from selling their shares to a third party unless the venture investors are offered the opportunity to sell at the same price. This is almost always required when the owner-managers have control of the company, to prevent the owners from receiving a premium for selling control and leaving venture investors with a minority illiquid interest in a business run by an unfamiliar third party.

Right of first offer, which is less severe than a right of first refusal and requires the seller to offer the shares to the company or the venture investors at a specified price before selling them to a third party at that price.

As in the case of a call, venture investors rarely grant a right of first refusal, take-along agreement, or right of first offer to owner-managers, because they limit upside potential by restricting the marketability of the venture investors' shares. However, venture investors usually are willing to provide contractual assurances that they will not sell to a third party when the owner-managers have reasonable objections—for example, a buyer who plans to liquidate the business or replace management.

Securities, Rights, and Remedies Venture Capitalists Receive

In certain situations, venture capitalists will invest their equity dollars in common stock side by side with owner-managers. However, as the earlier example illustrates, venture capitalists often prefer to invest the major portion of their equity dollars in securities which yield current income and have seniority to the securities issued to management. This is particularly true when the venture capitalist furnishes a large percentage of the equity dollars invested in the buyout.

It is common for the venture financing to be furnished as an investment in yield-bearing subordinated notes or redeemable preferred stock, with the venture investor's agreed-upon equity play represented by common stock purchased at the price per share management pays or by warrants or conversion rights to acquire common stock at that price. Under this typical structure, most of the venture investor's dollars are represented by rate-bearing securities which are junior to all other debt raised to finance the buyout but have liquidation preference over the common equity.

Even if the venture investors do not have economic or voting control, their financing agreements with the acquired company will provide them with the representations, covenants, and remedies they deem necessary to protect their investment. These usually include:

> Representations that all material information has been disclosed and that all financial statements, schedules, and other information provided are accurate.

The right to periodically inspect company property and receive detailed monthly financial statements and the annual operating budgets. Board representation or the right to attend all board and committee meetings.

Affirmative covenants requiring the company to maintain the operating condition of its properties and appropriate insurance, duly pay taxes and other obligations, and maintain its corporate existence.

Negative covenants limiting the company's ability to incur additional obligations, enter into new businesses, make acquisitions or merge or sell assets. (These covenants usually track those contained in senior financing documents.)

Restrictions on the company's ability to issue any class of security that is senior or have parity with the securities owned by the venture investors.

Restrictions on the company's ability to issue additional common stock which would be dilutive to the venture investors.

The right to require the company to register the venture-held common shares for public sale at the company's expense, usually after the company's first primary offering or after a reasonable period of time.

Restrictions on the sale of shares held by initial owner-managers, such as a right of first refusal, take-along agreement, or right of first offer discussed earlier.

Defaults under traditional venture financing agreements occur if the company breaches significant provisions of those agreements; fails to pay dividends, interest, or principal due on the venture-held securities; becomes insolvent or files for bankruptcy; or is in default of other material agreements.

However, the remedies venture investors may exercise upon the occurrance of a default are usually severely limited because their securities are junior to the senior lenders in a leveraged buyout. The most important remedy, the right to accelerate the due date of subordinated notes or redeemable preferred, can rarely be exercised while any senior debt is outstanding.

There are certain remedies customarily employed in venture financings which do not usually run afoul of senior debt agreements and are designed to motivate owner-managers to avoid or cure material defaults. These include (1) the right of the venture investors to take control of the board of directors; (2) a penalty in the form of an increase in the dividend or interest rate on the venture-held securities (while this usually only accrues, it acts as a penalty since it has preference over the owner-managers' common equity); and (3) the issuance of low-priced warrants to the venture investors which dilute the owner-managers' equity interest in the company.

One of the biggest challenges for an owner-manager in dealing with venture investors is negotiating and documentating the venture financing arrangements. Because of the high risk inherent in the securities they receive, venture capitalists have a penchant for protecting themselves against every contingency. While the owner-manager should carefully consider the risks and implications of providing significant rights and remedies to the venture investors, he must also understand that he's not being singled out nor is his word or integrity being questioned. Rather, it is the price of venture financing which is customary in virtually every similar transaction entered into by the venture investors.

BUSINESS AND FINANCIAL CHARACTERISTICS OF TARGET COMPANIES

A leveraged buyout, by its nature, increases the financial risk of the acquired business by subjecting it to significant additional debt, the proceeds of which are not invested in the company. This risk can be minimized by paying the right price for the business and adopting a sound financing structure. Venture capitalists generally prefer to finance leveraged buyouts which they believe present a relatively low business risk in relation to the reward they receive.

It is helpful to keep in mind two rules of thumb followed by most leveraged buyout specialists. First, the principal method of achieving equity appreciation is generating cash flow to pay down as rapidly as possible the debt used in the acquisition. It is generally not the intent to acquire a business in a leveraged financing and realize value by growing the business. Table 7–2 illustrates this point. A company bought for $20 million (using $4 million of equity and $16 million in debt) which generates sufficient cash flow to retire all acquisition debt in five years and is sold for the same $20 million at the end of that period will produce a compound annual rate of return of 38 percent to the equity investors. A sale for $30 million will produce a 50 percent return. If the acquisition financing is $3 million in equity and $17 million in debt, a sale in the fifth year for $20 million after all debt is repaid will result in a 46 percent return, and a sale for $30 million returns 58 percent to the equity investors. If the company's sale price doubles to $40 million and all debt is paid prior to a fifth year sale, the returns jump to 58 percent on a $4 million equity investment and 68 percent using $3 million in equity.

Second, while they may present attractive acquisition targets, busi-

TABLE 7–2 **Comparative Financing and Rate of Return for Company Purchased for $20 Million and Sold Five Years Later** ($ Thousands)

	Case 1	Case 2	Case 3
Financing conditions	$4 million equity, $16 million debt; all dept repaid prior to sale.	$3 million equity, $17 million debt; all debt repaid prior to sale.	Same as Case 2, but all debt repaid from sale proceeds.
Compound annual rate of return for sale price of:			
$20,000	38%	50%	58%
$30,000	46	58	68
$40,000	0	34	50

nesses which have prospects of growing rapidly are not generally suitable for leveraged acquisitions. Usually the seller can command a premium for future growth, reflected in a higher price earnings multiple. The higher price often results in insufficient earnings and cash flow to service debt. In addition, future growth means additional financing requirements for increases in receivables and inventory and for possible plant expansion and increased marketing expense. These additional financing demands are incompatible with an already highly leveraged balance sheet.

Accordingly venture capitalists generally will consider providing buyout financing for stable, low-growth businesses which have the following characteristics:

Management Team. A complete operating management team that has a proven track record with the target company should be in place. The quality of management is usually the most important element considered by venture capitalists evaluating a leveraged buyout. A new management team or an existing team with a poor track record presents unacceptable risks to most venture investors. As noted above, venture capitalists require key managers to invest a meaningful portion of their personal assets in the equity of the new company.

Products. A manufacturer or distributor should have products with a long product life cycle and little risk of technological change or obsolescence. Preferably the product line should have a proprietary aspect and a strong regional or national market position.

Plant/Equipment. The company's plants and equipment should be in good operating condition, and the company should have a history of making capital expenditures in excess of depreciation expense. Ideally, capital expenditure requirements in the critical early years of the buyout should be minimal.

Historic Cash Flow. The company should have a history of stable cash flow generation with low working capital requirements, available capacity to accommodate sales growth, and the demonstrated ability to increase prices to cover inflationary cost increases.

No Contingent Surprises. There should be no known contingent events which could put a strain on the company's cash flow, such as a large labor contract which expires shortly, threatened litigation, potential environmental cleanup obligations, or an excessive unfunded pension liability.

No Turnarounds. While turnaround situations can present attractive investment opportunities, venture capitalists generally will not combine the business risk of successfully effecting a turnaround with the financial risk of highly leveraging the company's balance sheet.

Asset Write-Up. The opportunity should exist to write up the tax basis of assets acquired in the buyout to eliminate any premium paid over book value. This will reduce taxable earnings but increase cash flow as a result of additional depreciation and amortization charges and an increase in the value of starting inventories.

Other Cash-Generating Opportunities. A company which has the flexibility to reduce working capital levels quickly, sell fixed assets which are not critical to operations, delay capital expenditures, or quickly reduce its labor expense can decrease the leverage risk during an economic downturn.

FINANCIAL STRUCTURE

The cornerstone to optimizing the financing component of the risk : reward ratio of a leveraged buyout is to choose experienced financial partners and a sound financial structure. Venture capitalists generally prefer lenders who have a history of financing leveraged buyouts and have demonstrated the capability to act rationally during adverse economic periods. These qualities are far more important than obtaining the best loan pricing.

The appropriate balance between debt and equity financing depends upon, among other things, the business and financial characteristics of the company being acquired in the buyout and the prevailing and anticipated interest rate and economic environment. The financial structure should be flexible enough to permit the company to weather sharp increases in interest rates and business downturns of reasonable severity.

The following general parameters are typical of buyouts being financed in today's environment by responsible venture capital groups:

- A ratio of senior debt plus subordinated debt to equity of less than 7:1.
- A ratio of senior debt to subordinated debt plus equity of less than 3.5:1.
- Interest rate coverage in the critical first full year of the buyout projected to be greater than 1.5:1 and increasing in each subsequent year (interest rate coverage = income before interest and taxes divided by the interest expense).
- Projected cash flow sufficient to pay scheduled debt repayments without sale of assets needed in the business.

The financing agreements should be tailored to the unique characteristics of the leveraged buyout. Covenants containing net worth and working capital maintenance tests should provide sufficient latitude to avoid triggering a default unless the lender's principal is truly endangered. In addition, the financing arrangements should provide necessary funding for anticipated working capital requirements. An interest rate cash cap, which in essence allows the company to add interest to loan principal if the rate exceeds a certain level, is a common technique to guard against a return to a 20 percent prime rate.

Venture capitalists generally opt for a financing structure that anticipates an adverse economic and interest rate environment. To get the necessary latitude from lenders usually requires an adequate equity base and a more conservative debt:equity ratio. For the safety inherent in an adequately capitalized buyout, venture capitalists will generally trade off the potentially higher returns achievable with an excessively leveraged balance sheet. By following this philosophy, experienced venture capitalists have historically achieved annual returns in excess of 35 percent, and very few of their buyouts have failed.

PURCHASE PRICE

The purchase price to be paid for a company acquired in a leveraged buyout is probably the most important determinant of whether the

TABLE 7–3 **Income after Interest Payments and before Taxes for First Year of Buyout** ($ Thousands)

Purchase price in multiples of pretax preinterest income	Acquisition debt	Case 1*		Case 2†	
		Interest rate 15 percent	Interest rate 18 percent	Interest rate 15 percent	Interest rate 18 percent
$20,000 (5X)	$16,000	$1,600	$ 1,120	$ 800	$ 320
$24,000 (6X)	19,200	1,120	544	320	(256)
$28,000 (7X)	22,400	640	(32)	(160)	(832)
$32,000 (8X)	25,600	160	(608)	(640)	(1,408)

* Case 1: Pretax, preinterest income is $4,000 for first year of buyout.
† Case 2: Pretax, preinterest income drops 20 percent to $3,200 for first year of buyout.

buyout can succeed. The best management team, soundest financing structure, and most experienced financing partners can't compensate for paying too high a price.

Since a company acquired in a leveraged buyout must rely on the cash flow it can generate to service its acquisition debt, the purchase price that can be paid is a function of future expected cash flow. In determining the correct purchase price, the buyer must make allowances for two contingencies over which he has no control: increases in interest rates and an adverse economic environment. The purchase price paid and the financing structure adopted must allow a sufficient cushion to service acquisition debt in the event these contingencies occur.

Table 7–3 illustrates the sensitivity of varying acquisition prices to two different interest rate and earnings levels. As in the previous example, the company depicted has pretax, preinterest income of $4 million for the year preceding the buyout and is to be acquired using a debt : equity ratio of 4 : 1. For example, at a multiple of five times pretax, preinterest income, the purchase price is $20 million, financed with $16 million of debt and $4 million of equity. The purchase price is analyzed in terms of multiples of the previous year's pretax, preinterest income, because this represents the expected cash flow source to service acquisition debt (assuming the company has no extra assets to sell and noncash charges such as depreciation are offset by capital expenditures). The table also illustrates the company's projected income after interest payments and before taxes for the first year of the buyout under varying purchase price scenarios, assuming interest rates of 15 percent and 18 percent and pretax, preinterest income levels of $4 million and $3.2 million.

The company's projected income after interest payments and before taxes is important because it represents the company's available cushion for further increases in interest rates or decreases in earnings. It is also the source of repayment of acquisition debt after applying the prevailing tax rate. At a multiple of five times the company's previous year's pretax, preinterest income, the company can weather both an increase in interest rates to 18 percent and a 20 percent drop in pretax, preinterest income to $3.2 million. At a multiple of six times, the company can survive an increase in interest rates to 18 percent or a 20 percent drop in pretax, preinterest income, but not both. At multiples of seven and eight, the company has no cushion to weather either a 20 percent rise in interest rates or a 20 percent drop in earnings.

The conclusion is clear: To pay a higher multiple than five times pretax, preinterest income leaves the company at significant risk if interest rates increase 20 percent or earnings drop by that amount.

Paying too high a multiple of pretax earnings not only increases the financial risk of the company's balance sheet through increased acquisition debt, but it also requires the company to experience real earnings growth to merely service its debt. In addition, achieving the investors' targeted return on investment will be dependent on the future sale of the company at the same or a higher multiple of earnings. For these reasons, it is often difficult to compete with other buyers who are not seeking to acquire the company on a leveraged basis and therefore will not be constrained in their purchase offer by the target company's cash flow–generating ability.

One effective way to reduce the purchase price is to make a purchase offer which includes seller financing. A seller will usually consider subsidizing the purchase price by providing favorable financing if he is under time pressure to sell or cannot receive a higher cash purchase price. If the seller is a public company, it may wish to avoid or minimize a write-off and therefore be willing to accept a large portion of the purchase price in the form of securities issued by the company it is selling.

The most attractive seller financing usually takes the form of subordinated notes or preferred stock. Generally these securities bear a below-market interest or dividend rate relative to the risk they represent and will have a fairly long maturity. The advantages of this type of financing to the buyer are several. These securities will be junior to senior debt, thereby increasing the leverage capacity of the acquired company. They decrease the financial risk of the buyout because they carry below-market fixed rates which are not affected by rising interest rates. In addition they represent a true reduction in the purchase price since they are priced to yield a return which is not commensurate with their risk level. However, to the extent they are in fact priced below market value the seller may have to write their carrying value down to market, thus recognizing a loss on the sale.

SELECTING AND APPROACHING VENTURE FIRMS

During the 1970s, venture subsidiaries of large bank holding companies were the principal venture leveraged buyout specialists. In recent years venture affiliates of insurance companies and investment banks, as well as privately managed venture partnerships, have become major buyout financiers.

Once a prospective buyer decides venture financing is appropriate, selecting the venture firm to lead the equity financing may be the most important decision he will make. He should use as much due diligence in making this selection as he does in choosing the business to buy. He is forming a five- to seven-year partnership. He should personally interview the principals of several venture firms. Get a list of *all* companies they've financed in leveraged buyouts, not just the successful ones. Ask which ones have gone well and which haven't. Talk to the managers of these companies to determine what kind of support the venture firm has provided in both good and bad times. Also interview banks and other lenders who have financed buyouts the venture firm has sponsored.

Quality venture firms will willingly undergo this type of scrutiny for an attractive financing opportunity. It is the same due diligence they are used to performing in evaluating investments. Experienced financing partners who don't panic during adverse times can make the difference between success and failure in a leveraged buyout.

Once the prospective buyer has narrowed his selection, it is best to concentrate on one firm at a time. Like any good businessman, venture firms do not like competition. Many venture firms will not participate in a bidding war. If the prospective buyer involves several venture firms and plans to shop for the best pricing, none of them may seriously consider the proposal. This is not to say the prospective buyer should not try to achieve the best deal possible. Rather he should learn from his own due diligence investigation which venture firms will provide a fair offer and should make it clear that he is giving the firm he chooses a first shot at the transaction but will move on to another firm if they cannot reach a mutually satisfactory arrangement.

It is also important to provide a realistic time frame in which to evaluate and close a transaction. When presented with an investment proposal which requires a quick yes-or-no decision, most venture firms will give the no go. Generally, the short time table is a sign of poor planning and incomplete due diligence by the presenter. Realistically, a venture firm that is presented with a fairly complete business plan, including detailed financial statements and projections, can give a strong indication of interest within a week. An extra two to four weeks should be allowed for the firm to meet management, visit plants, talk with suppliers and customers, and complete its industry due diligence.

After the prospective owner and venture firm reach agreement, it then can take anywhere from two to six additional weeks to negotiate the purchase with the seller, arrange and negotiate the other financing arrangements, complete legal due diligence, perform special audits if required, and finalize all legal documentation. It is unrealistic to close a typical leveraged buyout involving a venture capital firm in less than eight weeks from start to finish.

Chapter 8

The Art of the ESOP Leveraged Buyout*
Joseph S. Schuchert

THE ESOP

Since the enactment of the Employee Retirement Income Security Act (ERISA) in late 1974, dozens of articles and commentaries and more than a half-dozen books have been published on the subject of employee stock ownership plans (ESOPs). Dissertations about ESOPs have been written by lawyers, accountants, investment bankers, commercial bankers, professors, actuaries, employee benefit consultants, insurance agents, appraisers, and others. ESOPs and the companies that have adopted them have been studied, analyzed, assessed, described, and compared in all manner of publications. Surveys have been conducted by universities, governmental agencies, and at least one congressional committee, seeking to probe and quantify the performances of ESOP companies.

Commentary on ESOPs has ranged from sharply critical to simplistically euphoric. Their characteristics have been described as "foibles" and "fables." They are imbued with "magic" in one book title and with "triumph" in another. Although most of what has been written is positive, the claims of detractors persist. The conflict is hardly surprising. Advocates too often have used a "shotgun" approach by recommending an ESOP solution as the remedy for every conceivable corporate problem, financial or otherwise. For example, the literature suggests that ESOPs can be designed to accomplish a litany of objectives, such as:

---

* Copyright 1984, Joseph S. Schuchert.

Raise additional capital.

Recapture taxes.

Assure estate liquidity.

Retire outstanding shares.

Provide a market for closely held stock.

Discourage unionization.

Buy out dissident stockholders.

Acquire other companies.

Combat tender offers.

Broaden the appeal of unions.

Shelter excess accumulated earnings.

Refinance existing debt.

Maximize IRS investment tax credit.

Divest subsidiaries.

Purchase key man insurance.

These purposes seem to be related only indirectly to the primary purpose required under ERISA for all employee benefit plans—that the best interest of the employees must always be paramount. The controversy over the potential uses of ESOPs centers not on whether they are possible but whether they are consistent with what has been called the "ERISA principle." This is the embodiment of all the requirements which ERISA and the Internal Revenue Code have made to ensure the safety of plan assets. Therefore, it seems appropriate first to consider and dispose of this very basic question.

The ESOP and the ERISA Principle

The apparent conflict between the ERISA principle and the use of the ESOP as an investment banking device has been a disquieting influence on many of those now counted as ESOP critics. Some always seem to foresee circumstances which are sure to lead to difficulties, if not disaster. Sensitivity to the restraints embodied in the ERISA principle can hardly be condemned. Since it is necessary to prevent fraud, self-dealing, or fundamental unfairness by ESOP fiduciaries, no one seriously objects to such proscriptions.

The basic question is whether ESOP corporate finance techniques inherently conflict with the standards imposed by the ERISA principle. If they do, the resulting incompatibility would probably demand that the ESOP statutory provisions be removed from ERISA and enacted in another body of legislation, perhaps one dealing with capital financing. Although this indeed would be a salutary improvement, it goes far beyond the bounds of the problem.

The author's experience in hundreds of cases confirms that investment banking applications of the ESOP are consistent with ERISA *as it applies to ESOPs.* Since ERISA defines the standard of conduct imposed upon fiduciaries, the special character and purpose of an ESOP should be the major factor in evaluating the prudence of an ESOP fiduciary. This special character and purpose become clear in the context of the historical concepts from which the ESOP emerged and which provided the foundation for much of the ensuing legislation giving it special status.

The origin of the ESOP lies in the writings of Louis O. Kelso, who in a series of books and articles argued the case of broadened capital ownership. Since the function of technological progress is to change from labor intensive to capital intensive the way in which goods and services are produced, it is imperative, said Kelso, that the way in which individuals participate in production and earn income also become capital oriented. But since conventional financing techniques give preferred—if not exclusive—access to capital credit to people who already are capital owners, it is necessary to invent a new approach to providing access to capital credit to the majority who own no capital.

In *The Capitalist Manifesto,* published in 1958, and in *The New Capitalists,* published in 1961, Kelso pointed out that the logic of capital acquisition has always been based upon the expectation that a newly acquired asset would earn enough, within an acceptable period of time, to pay off its acquisition costs. Thereafter, it would produce net income for its new owners. But the feasibility risk—the risk that the new asset might not liquidate its purchase costs within the expected period of time—had, for whatever reason, historically been self-insured by the entrepreneur acquiring the asset. This resulted in limiting access to capital credit to those already owning substantial capital. Clearly, argued Kelso, the income-earning power of capital cannot be made accessible to persons wholly dependent upon their labor power by financing methods that are destined, deliberately or not, to make the rich richer. Such techniques are useless to the capitalless.

To meet this problem, in 1956 (two years before publication of *The Capitalist Manifesto*) Kelso invented the ESOP (the name came later) to enable the employees of a small newspaper chain in Palo Alto, California, to buy the business from the retiring owner and to pay for it out of its pretax earnings, without requiring any payroll deductions or investment of their mostly nonexistent savings. Kelso "created" the ESOP by modifying the stock bonus plan, which had enjoyed tax-exempt status since 1921. To do this, he secured Treasury rulings recognizing the right of such plans to borrow and purchase employer stock. This change permitted the ESOP to become a corporate finance tool. More specifically, the ESOP became that long-missing credit device that enabled people without savings or capital—in this case, corporate employees—to buy employer stock and to pay for it out of the pretax earnings of the assets represented by that stock. Furthermore, after the assets have been paid for, the employees become the owners without the earnings used to liquidate the debt having been subjected to the personal income taxes of the employees.

Since 1973, four separate administrations have signed into law 15 bills promoting the use of ESOPs as a means to expand the ownership of productive capital, while providing a method of greatly increasing the efficiency of corporate earnings used for capital purposes. The legislation is replete with references to the ESOP as a "technique of corporate finance." In addition, in the Tax Reform Act of 1976, Congress took the unusual step of specifying its intent and cautioning the regulatory agencies not to frustrate it:

> The Congress, in a series of laws . . . has made clear its interest in encouraging employee stock ownership plans as a bold and innovative method of strengthening the free private enterprise system which will solve the dual problems of securing capital funds for necessary capital growth and of bringing about stock ownership by all corporate employees. The Congress is deeply concerned that the objectives sought by this series of laws will be made unattainable by regulations and rulings which treat employee stock ownership plans as conventional retirement plans, which reduce the freedom of employee trusts and employers to take the necessary steps to implement the plans, and which otherwise block the establishment and success of the plans.

It would be difficult to cite a clearer statement of legislative intent on any subject. Historical evidence and legislative history therefore establish the special character and purpose of the ESOP as a simultaneous technique of corporate finance—primarily an investment banking tool and a very efficient credit mechanism to enable employees to buy stock and pay for it out of the pretax earnings of the assets represented by that stock.

As a creature of statute, the ESOP is mandated to invest *primarily* in company stock. As a general proposition, therefore, any fair market value purchase of company stock by the ESOP fulfills its special purpose. That the corporation, its stockholders, or others may reap substantial gains does not violate the ERISA principle. One of the delights of creative, responsible ESOP use is the ability to complete transactions of an investment banking nature which benefit all—employees, corporations, and stockholders. Indeed, it is a totally grotesque interpretation of the ESOP to expect it to be beneficial *only* to employees. To be an employee is to have many powerful and important invisible ties to others with whom your economic well-being becomes linked. The corporation in which you acquire stock becomes partly owned by you. What injures or benefits it injures or benefits you.

ESOP as a Financing Vehicle

For those not acquainted with the nature and basic operations of the conventional ESOP, a brief description is appropriate. In technical terms, an ESOP is a stock bonus or combination stock bonus and money purchase plan "qualified" under the Internal Revenue Code. A plan is qualified if it complies with the various participation, vesting, distribution, and other rules established by ERISA to protect the interests of the employees. An ESOP is thus classified as a type of retirement plan to which corporate payments may be made with full tax deductibility. Further, an employee is not currently taxed on payments made to his account in the ESOP until his capital account is distributed to him (usually upon retirement or termination of employment), and then at capital gain rates.

Certain characteristics unique to the ESOP make it adaptable as a method of corporate finance. An employee stock ownership trust, which is the administrative entity for an ESOP, is required to invest primarily in the securities of the employer corporation. In order to purchase such securities, the ESOP is permitted to borrow money, and the corporation is permitted to guarantee such loans.

An ESOP which utilizes borrowed funds to purchase securities is termed a *leveraged* ESOP. It may be employed either to purchase shares from the corporation, and thereby finance an expansion of the business, or to facilitate a transfer of ownership of the corporation, commonly referred to as a buyout. In either case, the loan to the ESOP is amortized with the payments the employer corporation makes to the ESOP.

In an ESOP leveraged transaction, the corporation may more efficiently amortize the loan out of pretax income of the business, since the corporation's payments are fully tax deductible. In a conventional loan, only interest is deductible by the borrowing corporation. Assuming an effective income tax rate of 50 percent, the corporation would have to earn approximately $20 million pretax to amortize the principal of a $10 million loan. Pretax income of only $10 million is needed to amortize the $10 million principal of the loan through an ESOP. Thus cash flow to service acquisition debt is increased substantially in a properly structured ESOP.

The key to a leveraged buyout is the dual capacity of the ongoing business to amortize its acquisition debt while simultaneously, with-

---

FIGURE 8–1   **Conventional Leveraged ESOP**

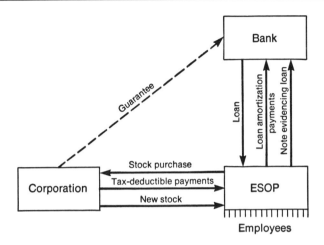

out additional investment, generating stock ownership in employees without their being taxed on it. (See Figure 8–1.) ESOP financing techniques materially enhance the prospect of success of a leveraged buyout while extending the excitement of capital acquisition to all employees. In fact, they make possible transactions otherwise impracticable because of inadequate cash flow and motivation that reaches only key executives but not the entire employee team.

Moreover, the use of an ESOP in such a transaction has the potential for improving employee stability, dedication, earning power, and capital well-being. This has been confirmed by a number of surveys, including those conducted by the University of Michigan, UCLA, the Department of State, the state of Maryland, and the Senate Finance Committee (SFC). Although a report of the General Accounting Office[1] and an article entitled "The Uneven Record of Employee Ownership"[2] question whether there is sufficient evidence to establish a reliable relationship between employee ownership and productivity, the SFC survey speaks strongly to the contrary. It draws its data entirely from ESOP companies and compares the performance of the businesses sampled for three-year periods, both before and after ESOP implementation. The results of the SFC survey appear in Table 8–1.

THE LEVERAGED BUYOUT

Characteristics

Typical leveraged buyout transactions generally involve one of the following:

TABLE 8-1   Performance Comparisons of All Corporations versus ESOP Samples: 1976-78* (Current Dollar Totals for the Years 1976, 1977, 1978)

	All corporations	ESOP sample†
Sales change percent	$529 billion† +39%	$1.064 billion +72%
Employment change percent change	9.5 million‡ +12%	12.3 thousand +37%
Profit change percent	71.8 billion +75%	93.4 million +157%
Tax change percent	34.7 billion +70%	35.1 million +150%
Tax rate	51%	38%
Productivity	+5.7%‡	+25%‖
Percent profit/sales	5.4%§	6.04%#

* Estimated dates of latest three-year data reported in SFC sample of 75 companies.
† Average ESOP in sample was three years old and 21 percent employee owned.
‡ Nonfarm.
§ All manufacturing.
‖ Based on sales per employee.
Pre-ESOP the profit/sales rate was 4.05 percent.
Sources: *1980 Economic Report of the President;* ESOP Sample from U.S. Senate Finance Committee, 1979.

---

1. The private company whose principals desire or need liquidity for estate planning, retirement, or other reasons.
2. The corporation seeking to sell off assets that no longer fit corporate product line strategies or meet the financial criteria of earnings growth or returns.
3. The public company desiring to "go private" because of limited or no access to capital markets, perceptions of undeservedly low stock market valuations, lack of liquidity for major stockholders, vulnerability of the business to corporate raiders, or other objectives incompatible with operating as a public company.

Prior to the 1960s, the sellers of businesses looked almost exclusively to larger corporations as logical buyers, since only they had sufficient cash or credit to handle cash buyouts. The 1960s was the time of public offerings and pooling arrangements. During the 1970s, many larger corporations lacked both the liquidity and credit to easily accommodate large purchases for cash. However, the need of the private corporate owner for a market for his stock continued to persist.

The collapse of the public market and the reduction in capital gains tax combined to make sales for cash acceptable.

The conglomerate movement focused on short-term earnings objectives rather than long-term financial and diversification goals. Anticipated increases in earnings per share turned out to be illusory, and management often found it difficult to properly understand, much less manage, such diverse businesses. Large corporations tended to become sellers rather than buyers. The era of divestitures commenced.

In the early 1970s, the leveraged buyout phenomenon began in earnest. The idea of buying assets with leverage has been around for decades, but the real action began with the unprecedented wave of corporate spin-offs in 1971 and 1972. Leveraged buyouts seem to continue even in uncertain times. They are now generally accepted as legitimate, even desirable tools of investment banking. Of course, a major factor underlying their success has been inflation, which has contributed to the soundness of asset-based lending.

Moreover, there is the growing realization among those participating in leveraged buyout activity that such purchases closely resemble real estate transactions when they involve established businesses, proven cash flows, and often undervalued asset bases. In the real estate field, leverage has always been considered desirable. An increasing number of lenders and investors have come to believe that leveraged business acquisitions can have the qualities of real property acquisitions—low risk, high return, and enormous upside potential.

Cyclically high interest rates obviously will deter many purchases. However, most transactions are structured to amortize acquisition debt over 5 to 15 years. Much of the acquisition debt now fluctuates with the prime rate, and lenders know from experience that interest rates will cycle several times during such a long period. In the case of ESOP leveraged buyouts, the tax deductibility of payments on principal tends to offset the adverse effect of high interest.

Role of the ESOP in Leveraged Buyouts

Normally the ESOP is integrated into the financial plan for a leveraged acquisition to form capital from the pretax income of the business acquired. As previously mentioned, the effect is substantially increased cash flow during the debt amortization period. The anatomy of an ESOP leveraged buyout can best be described in the context of a hypothetical transaction. A nontechnical definition of the ESOP, supplied by the author, will help to visualize its function: The ESOP is (1) a technique of corporate financing which (2) allows deductible payments by a corporation to an employee trust (3) for the purchase of stock for the accounts of employees (or the repayment of loans used to purchase such stock) (4) from the corporation or from existing stockholders or both (5) at fair market value. Applying this description, it will be helpful to think of the ESOP as the "black box" integrated into the corporate finance system through which deductible corporate payments flow to finance purchases of company stock.

A typical ESOP acquisition structure may be illustrated by this hypothetical case. Diversified Business, Inc. decides to divest its wholly owned subsidiary Alpha Corporation because its return on investment falls short of corporate objectives developed after a recent change of top management. Alpha is a manufacturer of telephone cable and coaxial cable, distributing its products in both the domestic and international markets. It has a proven earnings performance, with real growth of 10 percent annually. It shares a strong market position primarily with three other manufacturers. The management team is of high quality, both from an operational and financial perspective.

Diversified has been discouraged by its attorneys from offering to sell Alpha to other cable manufacturers because of possible antitrust repercussions. Moreover, with competitors ruled out as prospective buyers, the market for such a specialized business is limited and may not produce a purchase price as high as the book value which Diversified desires to receive. In addition, Diversified would like to avoid the loss of Alpha's management or a decline in operating efficiency resulting from the potentially demoralizing information that Alpha is "on the block." Diversified elects to consider an ESOP leveraged buyout proposal recommended by an investment banking firm and by members of Alpha's management, who will form Beta Corporation to make the acquisition.

The parameters of the proposed leveraged acquisition by Alpha's management group are as follows:

Type of business:	Manufacturer of telephone and coaxial cable.
Sales:	$60 million.
Pretax income:	$6 million.
Tax rate:	50 percent.
Net profit after taxes:	$3 million.
Net worth:	$20 million.
Number of employees:	800.
Payroll—ESOP participants:	$12 million.
Pension expense:	$1 million.

Purchase price: $20 million—$15 million in cash
                                   and $5 million in notes.

Capitalization of Beta Corporation will be handled as follows:

Senior debt: $15 million seven-year secured note from bank at 1½ percent over prime.

Subordinated debt: $5 million 15 percent subordinated seven-year note to seller. No principal payment during first two years, level principal thereafter.

Equity: $700,000 (of which $500,000 is from management group and $200,000 from investment banker) purchases 25,000 shares and 10,000 shares respectively of Class B common stock. This represents 100 percent of Class B common and is convertible into 35 percent of Class A common on a fully diluted basis. Class B common is subordinated to Class A common and has dividend rights equal to one 10th of Class A common.

ESOP purchases 65,000 shares of Class A common stock, initially 100 percent of Class A shares, for $13 million. The source of the funds is a loan from a Beta subsidiary to the ESOP. These shares will become 65 percent of common when and if Class B common converts into Class A.

The above scenario for the ESOP leveraged acquisition of Alpha would involve the steps outlined in Figure 8–2.

1. Organization.   Key management employees of Alpha organize a new corporation, Beta Corporation (Beta), with an authorized capital of 100,000 shares of Class A and 35,000 shares of Class B common stock. A wholly owned Beta subsidiary (Beta Sub) would also be organized.

2. Classes of Stock.   Class A common stock is senior to Class B common stock in dividend and liquidation rights. Class B common, or "founders," stock is purchased by management members at a much lower price than Class A. Upon the attainment of specified financial objectives, Class B is converted into Class A, thus eventually increasing the value of the equity held by management. Of course, failure to achieve the stipulated financial goals means that founders stock will not convert into the much more valuable, senior Class A stock. This device thus places a clear performance burden on management. Indeed, the success that triggers the promotion of founders stock also enhances the value of the ESOP's Class A stock.

FIGURE 8–2

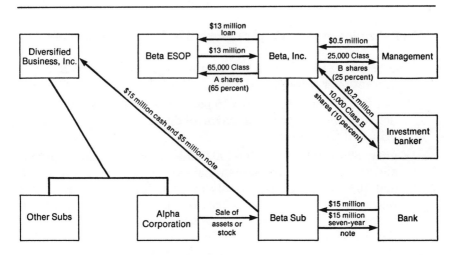

3. Installation of ESOP. Upon the organization of Beta, an ESOP would be carefully designed to optimize all aspects of this unique device and, after due consideration, would be adopted. In Internal Revenue terms, it would be a leveraged stock bonus plan which would permit Beta Sub to finance through its amounts equivalent to 25 percent of the covered payroll of ESOP participants, plus interest on any debt incurred by the ESOP.

4. Financing Arrangements. Of the $20 million purchase price, $15 million would be borrowed by Beta Sub from commercial banks. The balance of $5 million would be financed by the seller, Diversified. Of the $15 million borrowed from banks, $13 million (or 65 percent of the purchase price) would be reloaned by Beta Sub to the Beta ESOP. The ESOP would use $13 million to buy 65,000 shares of Beta Class A common stock—initially 100 percent of the Class A common stock and 65 percent on a fully diluted basis. This loan will be amortized in annual installments of $3 million each for the first three years and $2 million each in the final two years.

5. Acquisition of Business and Assets of Alpha. Beta, Beta Sub, and Diversified would enter into an agreement for the sale of the assets or stock of Alpha to Beta Sub for $20 million. The former employees of Alpha would become employees of Beta Sub and participants in the Beta ESOP.

6. Amortization of Acquisition Debt. After conclusion of the sale of the business, Beta Sub would make payments each year to the Beta ESOP sufficient to provide for payments of principal and interest on the loan to the ESOP.

Observations and Comments

The hypothetical leveraged buyout of Alpha is, of course, only one of many ways the acquisition could have been structured. It illustrates an approach which has been followed in a number of transactions. Some observations and comments, however, are important.

1. Cash Flow. ESOP financing alone generates additional cash flow of $6.5 million over the first five years, resulting from tax savings on ESOP payments. Annual payments of $3 million (25 percent of payroll) for three years and $2 million (17 percent of payroll) for the next two years shield $13 million of pretax income from taxes, which would otherwise have totaled $6.5 million. In addition, pension plan contributions of $1 million per year are suspended, increasing pretax income by $5 million over the five-year period. Income taxes would consume $2.5 million, leaving $2.5 million to net income. Thus a total of $9 million in additional cash flow is injected into the new company, which will permit it to amortize its acquisition debt much more rapidly.

Normally, the company guarantees that the employees' retirement income will never be less than it would have been had pension plan contributions not been suspended. Since total ESOP payments of $13 million over the five-year period are almost triple the suspended $5 million in aggregate pension payments, such an assurance appears reasonable.

2. Management Stock. Experience in a number of ESOP leveraged acquisitions has reinforced the desirability of providing key members of the management group with the opportunity to acquire substantial ownership in addition to their participation in the ESOP. Obviously, additional motivation is important, especially where the business is highly leveraged and the need to hold executive salaries and fringes to a minimum is essential.

Beyond motivation, however, is the magnitude of the undertaking and the commitment demanded of the key management group in connection with the transaction itself. First, success or failure of the ongoing business will have a profound effect on the career paths of key executives. Failure of the business, for whatever reasons, could be very detrimental to future career opportunities. Second, banks, financial institutions, and investors providing capital for the transaction may require key management people personally to guarantee some portion of these loans. At a minimum, they will often be required to sign employment agreements binding them to the corporation over a period of years, thus blocking other career opportunities.

Employees whose services to the business are less unique, and who therefore are not part of the group, are not similarly affected. The failure of the business ordinarily will not influence their future job opportunities. Individually, they will carry no stigma because of the corporation's demise. And they are never required to guarantee debt or enter into employment agreements. Accordingly, astute management teams are reluctant to take on these added risks and burdens without a quid pro quo. The objective is to provide the management members the opportunity, predicated upon the success of the ongoing business, to acquire at reasonable cost a substantial interest in the corporation in addition to ESOP participation.

The Economic Recovery Act of 1981 provided for a liberalized arrangement for stock options which can be used as a part of the management ownership package. However, the limitation of $100,000 per executive participant detracts considerably from their usefulness as a replacement for founders stock in a leveraged buyout.

3. Bank Loans to Corporation. In this transaction, the bank loan was made to the Beta Corporation rather than to the ESOP. Also, the ESOP was not a party to the subordinated note paid to Diversified. Beta Corporation, in turn, makes a loan to its ESOP. The corporation is entitled to a tax deduction for all interest payments plus all ESOP contributions.

In many leveraged buyout transactions, the financial institutions seek to hold all of the stock of the ongoing business as collateral until the loans are repaid. But the regulations covering ESOP loans require the stock of the employer corporation which is purchased with loan proceeds to be released proportionately from the collateral as the loan is amortized. Accordingly, the Alpha case uses both a holding company and a wholly owned subsidiary. The ESOP is adopted by the parent corporation, and its securities are sold to, and held by, the ESOP.

However, the business is acquired by the wholly owned subsidiary, whose stock is pledged to the banks as collateral, free of any regulatory restrictions. The ESOP and all other shareholders own the stock of the holding company. The bank holds as collateral all of the stock of the operating subsidiary, thus enjoying an ability to sell or appropriately deal with the subsidiary in the event of default.

4. Why Not Lend to the ESOP? Prior to FASB Statement of Position 76–3 (SOP 76–3) in 1976, one of the major attractions of ESOP financing was that loans to the ESOP by the financial institution were not liabilities on the balance sheet of the employer corporation. The company guarantee of the ESOP loan was merely footnoted as a contingent liability. If the loan proceeds were used to purchase newly issued securities, equity was correspondingly increased. SOP 76–3 changed this treatment dramatically by requiring the corporation to carry the liability on its balance sheet, even if no corporate guarantee is involved.

Unfortunately the required accounting treatment distorts the financial condition of a corporation with a borrowing ESOP. This treatment fails to distinguish a direct loan obligation, amortized from after-tax income, from an ESOP loan obligation amortizable through wholly deductible payments. Moreover, it is difficult to understand how an ESOP loan can be distinguished from a corporate obligation to a defined benefit pension plan having a large unfunded liability. In either case, the corporation must make payments to enable the plan to meet its liabilities. The magnitude of the plan obligation is defined in either situation. The argument for booking the present value of the unfunded liability of the pension plan on the balance sheet has some validity, since the Pension Benefit Guaranty Corporation (PBGC) has a claim against the corporation for up to 30 percent of its net worth should PBGC be required to pay retirement claims.

Of course, these and other arguments have all been made over the years. Nevertheless, SOP 76–3 remains in effect. Financial institutions prefer to lend to the corporation rather than to the ESOP. Their officers are uneasy about lending to an ESOP trustee acting as a fiduciary for employees. If the ESOP pledges company stock purchased with the loan proceeds, the regulations mandate that the bank release shares from the collateral pledge as the loan is amortized. If a default occurs after more than one half of the loan has been paid off, the bank would be able to exercise control over only a minority interest in the corporation. Consequently, without the advantage of providing "off balance sheet" financing, these disadvantages may discourage direct ESOP loans.

5. The Valuation Problem.   Since the essence of a leveraged acquisition presumes that the purchase price has been arrived at as the result of arm's-length bargaining, the transaction normally may be considered to reflect the fair market value of the business. Due to the close relationship which often exists between the parties, a valuation review should be conducted to confirm this conclusion. In addition, in a "going private" leveraged buyout transaction, an independent committee appointed by the board of directors may be required to make a fairness recommendation on behalf of the stockholders. The purpose of this is to determine that the purchase price is not *less* than fair market value.

FIGURE 8-3

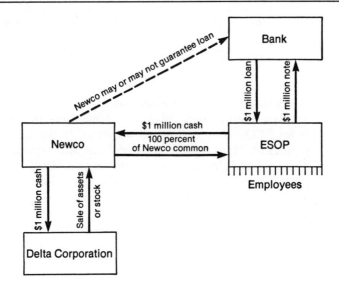

On the other hand, the company cannot sell its securities to its ESOP for *more* than fair market value, independently determined by the application of generally accepted criteria for the valuation of corporate securities. The value of the business purchased and the value of all of the stock of the ongoing corporation are identical. Considerable care must be taken to assure that the purchase price negotiated on behalf of the buyer can be fairly related to the valuation of the stock acquired by the ESOP in the ongoing corporation.

The requirement for a balancing of interest is somewhat complicated by the accounting treatment of the ESOP loan. This can best be illustrated by a hypothetical case. Figure 8-3 depicts the transaction with the bank loan directly to the ESOP only to demonstrate clearly the anomalous result. Presumably Newco has paid fair market value for the business and assets of Delta. The ESOP has provided the funds for the acquisition by purchasing all of the stock of Newco for $1 million. However, the instant the ESOP borrows the $1 million from the bank (whether or not the loan is guaranteed by Newco), an equivalent liability emerges on the Newco balance sheet. Although the stock proceeds have been used to purchase the business and assets of Delta, the net worth of Newco is reduced to zero. The ESOP has paid $1 million for Newco, which has no equity whatsoever at the conclusion of the transaction. Obviously, the conventional analyst will have considerable difficulty working his way through such a balance sheet to reach the proper value of Newco's stock.

The answer to the apparent dilemma lies in ignoring, for valuation purposes, the curious accounting treatment resulting from the application of SOP 76–3. The ESOP leveraged buyout transaction may be analogous to the purchase of an income-producing office building. Maximum leverage for such a transaction is normally considered a desirable objective. However, the mortgage loan taken to buy the property does not reduce or affect the market value of the building itself, even though it constitutes a lien on, and will be paid from, the income of the property. The mortgage is considered only as acquisition debt.

Similarly, if the ESOP loan is considered only as acquisition indebtedness, it should not result in the reduction of the *value* of the ESOP stock. It only represents the obligation undertaken for the acquisition, which reduces the *net worth of the ESOP but not, for appraisal purposes, the net worth of the business acquired.* As far as the corporation is concerned, the ESOP loan must be repaid from company payments into the ESOP only. The ESOP loan is not a claim against any assets of the ESOP trust except the stock purchased with its proceeds.

SEVERAL CASE STUDIES

It may now be useful to look at several case studies of ESOP leveraged buyouts. Clearly, they could have been packaged in a variety of other ways. All utilize the ESOP as a technique of corporate finance to build major ownership into the ESOP participants, and all provide for substantial economic opportunity to key management group members.

Case 1: Omega Apparel Corporation[3]

Omega Apparel Corporation is a quasi-public corporation having less than 500 shareholders and a very inactive market. It desires (1) to go private, cashing out the stockholders at a fair price significantly higher than market; (2) to provide liquidity for the major stockholder and his family, primarily for estate planning purposes; (3) to arrange for the key management group and the family of the controlling stockholder to participate in a substantial way in the future ownership of the business; and (4) to build new ownership into all employees of the enterprise in place of ownership by the public or other outsiders.

These objectives are being accomplished through an ESOP leveraged buyout based upon a tender offer from a newly organized corporation, Omega Corporation (Omega). Fifty percent of the outstanding common stock, in the form of Class B common (similar to that described in the hypothetical Alpha acquisition), is being issued to the selected man-

FIGURE 8–4

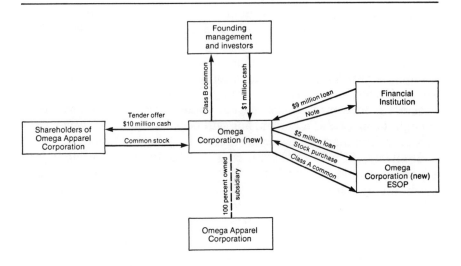

agement group and other investors for $1 million. The other 50 percent, in the form of Class A common, is being sold to the Omega ESOP for $5 million, equal to approximately one half the aggregate tender price. Bank financing of $9 million, based on a six-year term loan, will enable Omega to lend $5 million to the Omega ESOP to accommodate its purchase of Class A common. Upon completion of the tender offer, Omega Apparel Corporation will be a subsidiary of the parent Omega Corporation, and its employees will be covered by the Omega Corporation ESOP. The transaction is illustrated in Figure 8–4.

The changes of ownership accomplished by the transaction are as follows:

Category	Before buyout	After buyout*
Officers, directors, and their families	47.5%	40.0%
Employees	1.7	50.0
Outside public shareholders	50.8	0.0
Investment banker	0.0	10.0

* Assumes all Class B common stock of ongoing corporation has been converted to Class A.

The structure demonstrates the ability of the corporation to go private, cashing out all stockholders and providing the major stockholder, through a family trust, with substantial participation in the leveraged transaction. Presumably, when acquisition debt has been repaid, shares owned by the family trust will have at least equal, and probably greater, value than the stock which was sold.

Case 2: Pamida, Inc.

Pamida, Inc., a public company with its shares traded in the New York Stock Exchange, sold its business and substantially all of its assets in an ESOP leveraged transaction in early 1981. A new corporation, New Pamida, Inc., organized by management employees and the investment banker, paid almost $42 million in addition to assuming certain liabilities of the seller. Since the transaction involved the sale of assets at substantially below book value, Pamida was entitled to income tax refunds of about $8.4 million.

The net cash purchase price plus anticipated tax refunds produced approximately $5.20 per share of outstanding common stock. The buy-out transaction called for Pamida, after the closing, to offer to purchase any and all shares tendered for $6.00 cash per share. The principal stockholder and others, holding in the aggregate more than 40 percent of its outstanding shares, agreed not to tender any of their shares. The market for Pamida stock went as low as 2½ in early 1980; on the strength of the proposed sale, it moved as high as 5⅝ toward year-end.

After the sale of the business and with appropriate amendments to its corporate charter, Pamida became a closed-end, diversified management investment company, intending to invest exclusively in tax-exempt securities. The form of the transaction satisfied the personal income, investment, and liquidity needs of the major stockholder and his family, who held about 44 percent of Pamida's stock. By not tendering their shares, they avoided substantial capital gain taxes which would have resulted from their very low tax basis. Moreover, maintaining their interest in Pamida as a closed-end investment company, distributing most of its income on tax-exempt investments to stockholders, reduces the impact which income taxes have on persons in their relatively high tax bracket. The investment, diversification, liquidity, and relative ease of valuation which the investment company provided were also important for estate planning.

New Pamida was initially owned 100 percent by the New Pamida ESOP, which purchased 1.9 million shares of its common stock with the proceeds of a $19,019,000 interest-free loan from the corporation. The total financial requirements were about $41 million. Their sources were: $26 million in cash or cash equivalents purchased from Pamida (leaving Pamida with an operating cash balance of $1.4 million); $4.5 million in industrial revenue bonds; and the balance of $10.1 million from a portion of a $25 million, nine-year term loan from five commercial banks. See Figure 8–5. The investment banker purchased a 15-

FIGURE 8–5

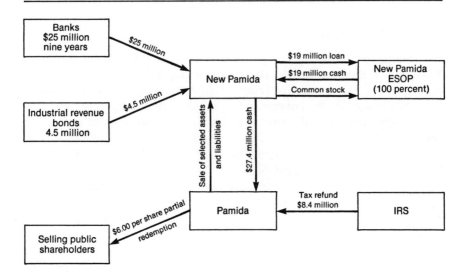

year warrant to purchase 8.5 percent of the corporation for about $10 per share. A generous cash bonus program, analogous to stock appreciation rights, was provided for members of the management group.

The overall transaction is unique in that it combines the ESOP financing technique, as applied to the debt amortization by the buyer, with the seller's ability to supplement the purchase price with a tax refund resulting from a sale of assets below book value. By keeping the aggregate proceeds (except those used to pay for shares tendered) in corporate solution and invested as a closed-end investment company, the objectives of the major stockholder were accommodated.

Case 3: Raymond International

Raymond International is an engineering and construction concern with 1982 revenues of $1.6 billion.

A new corporation, Raymond Holdings, Inc., was organized as the primary acquisition vehicle. The acquisition of the target operating company was funded by a combination of bank loans, cash equity, and the conversion of some of the assets of existing employee benefit plans to an ESOP. The operating company became a wholly owned subsidiary of the holding company, which is, in turn, owned primarily by the ESOP.

The funds for the purchase came from bank loans (roughly $180 million), an equity investment by management and Kelso, through Kelso Investment Associates, of about $5 million and $1.2 million respectively, in exchange for 100 percent of the Class B common in Raymond Holdings. And there was a conversion of certain assets held in employee benefit plans into an ESOP. The ESOP bought 100 percent of Raymond Holdings' common stock, Class A, with a note for approximately $100 million to that new corporation.

Conversion of employee benefit assets was an integral part of the financing, which was crucial to the success of this particular arrangement because it yielded a substantial amount of capital. Perhaps most important was the termination of the existing pension plan which affected 4,200 Raymond employees. In terminating the plan, the company was required to satisfy the obligation to assure that employees get what they have earned to date under the pension program. To accomplish this, it will buy a single-premium annuity from a major insurance company guaranteeing those earned benefits. Once that annuity is paid for, there will be nearly $30 million in excess pension funds that will revert to the company. Ordinarily, such excess funds would be taxable income. But under the terms outlined in the buyout plan, the company contributes all that money directly to the ESOP so that it becomes nontaxable. The ESOP then pays the money to Raymond Holdings to pay down its note, and that too is a nontaxable transaction.

Raymond also had a defined-contribution thrift plan which, on conversion, will produce about $21 million in cash that will acquire a block of Series A preferred in Raymond Holdings. Another $932,580 came from a stock bonus plan, and those funds purchased Series B preferred. Both preferred issues became part of the ESOP assets.

Through these transactions, the company was able to generate enough capital to make the leveraged buyout practicable. And because the ESOP operation so markedly improved cash flow, the chances of the company's healthy survival were geometrically increased.

Figure 8–6 shows how Raymond International went private. The means was a leveraged employee stock ownership plan which works this way: (1) ESOP buys 100 percent of Class A common and pays for it with a $100 million note. (2) Newly formed Raymond Holdings makes a tax-deductible contribution to the ESOP through the operating subsidiary. (3) The ESOP repays its note to Raymond Holdings with ESOP nontaxable funds. (4) Raymond Holdings funnels the note repayments through the operating subsidiary to the lenders, i.e., the banks.

A Theoretical Comparison: Houdaille Industries, Inc.

In 1979, a $356 million leveraged buyout of Houdaille Industries, Inc. was consummated—at that time, the largest ever done. The trans-

FIGURE 8-6

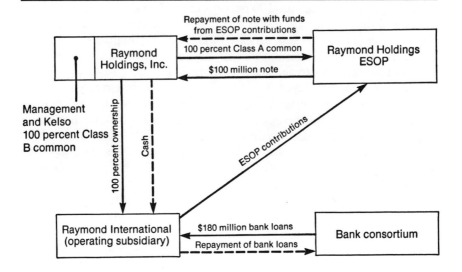

action was creatively structured by Kohlberg, Kravis, Roberts & Co., the investment banking firm responsible for several large leveraged buyouts usually employing the "cash merger" approach. From the proxy and other information available to the public, some observations can be made on possible differences in the Houdaille transaction had ESOP financing techniques been utilized to meet somewhat different objectives. Obviously, there may be factors, financial or otherwise, not apparent from the material available which would modify the comparison.

Utilization of an ESOP could enable ultimate ownership of the business to be structured in a substantially different way, as indicated below:

Common stock ownership	As consummated	Theoretical ESOP structure
Management	8%	25%
Institutional lenders	67	20–30
Investment banker	25	5
Employees	0	40–50

In addition, increased cash flows resulting from the ESOP approach would have reduced lender risks, permitting an even more highly leveraged capital structure. As consummated, the Houdaille buyout was achieved with an equity base of $51 million in the holding company, with new debt (in a subsidiary acquisition company) of $60 million in the form of a revolving credit agreement, $140 million of senior notes, and $104 million in subordinated debt. Utilizing an ESOP, the buyout could theoretically have been achieved with only $6 million in equity, new debt of $160 million in a revolving credit agreement, $70 million in senior notes, and $119 million in subordinated debt. An ESOP obligation of $22 million (18 percent of covered payroll) was assumed, and pension plan contributions of $6 million and $7 million were eliminated in the first two years. Due to the deductibility of ESOP payments, the cash flow under the ESOP scenario is markedly superior to that under the traditional approach, despite the higher level of debt and interest expense.

The equity participation allocated to institutions under the ESOP approach may or may not have been acceptable to them. However, net worth at the end of five years is projected to be approximately $180 million, assuming 100 percent growth in operating profit. A substantial portion of this equity is attributable to the purchase of new stock by the ESOP with deductible payments into the ESOP made by the company. Interest of only 10 percent per annum on the incremental cash generated would produce an additional net profit of $16.4 million in the five-year period. Thus, using ESOP financing, projected net worth at the end of 1983 would be about twice the approximately $100 million estimated under the actual structure used.

Consequently, while institutional lenders would own a smaller share of the company in the ESOP scenario, the value of their holdings after five years would approach that attained in the conventional buyout. Additionally, the increased cash flows enhance the soundness of their loans, which are also repaid more quickly.

KELSO AND THE ESOP

The leveraged buyouts described above apply many of the same principles as those originally structured by Louis Kelso in the 1950s. While some of the financing techniques have been refined, the substance of the concept remains: capital formation from corporate pretax income. In about 1970, Kelso gave the name of employee stock ownership plan (ESOP) to this financing device. It was no coincidence that Congress followed suit in 1973 when ERISA was enacted. It was only then that the term *employee stock ownership plan* attained special legal meaning and status and the ESOP movement began in earnest. But neither the ESOP nor the movement can be properly understood except in the context of Kelso's concept of democratized capitalism.

Kelso is truly a man of energy and vision. In his first book, written with Mortimer J. Adler and published in 1958, he argued that capitalism as currently practiced leads inevitably to ever increasing and so-

cially intolerable concentrations of wealth. This results from the application of conventional financing techniques which assure that the
owners of existing capital become the owners of newly created capital.

Kelso saw attempts to deal with the resulting inequities by redistribution of income through job programs, coercively rigging the price
of labor, progressive taxation, and transfer payments—as ineffective,
inflationary measures which lead society away from free enterprise
and towards increasing government intervention and eventual state
socialism. In Kelso's estimation, the economic democracy that pre-
vailed in the days of the founding fathers—where labor accounted for
95 percent of productive input and capital (primarily land) for only 5
percent—has been slowly replaced by an advanced industrial economy
in which, measured by now hypothetical market values of inputs into
production, capital accounts for at least 90 percent of input and labor
for no more than 10 percent. But capital ownership today is in the top 5
percent of the population, just as it was in 1789 when Benjamin Frank-
lin made that original estimate. The productiveness of capital today,
however, is thousands of times greater than it was in colonial times.
The economic democracy that once matched our political democracy
has been replaced by plutocracy that forces the economy to run on
redistributed income.

Most of the income attributable to capital is paid out to labor in the
form of wages and benefits as part of the redistribution process, rather
than the much smaller share which would accrue to it if the value of
labor were determined only by supply and demand in an unregulated
free market economy. In Kelso's view, the distortions and imbalances
thus created can only be corrected by providing an opportunity for
every family legitimately to acquire a capital estate through which it
can earn a significant and increasing portion of its income.

Kelso's ideas have evoked little positive response from establishment
economists, who tend to reject this two-factor analysis and go no further with a study of his ideas. This has not deterred Kelso, however,
who elected to begin a vigorous campaign for his theories with the
Congress of the United States. His determination and fevor have produced significant results. Since 1973, he has pursuaded Senators Rus-
sell Long, Mark Hatfield, and Ted Stevens, and many others both in
the Senate and the House, of the merits of his ideas for creating new
capitalists. Congress has approved 15 pieces of legislation promoting
the use of ESOPs; four administrations have signed them into law.

Author's Postscript

I first met Louis Kelso in late 1969 when he interviewed me for a job
as an attorney with his law firm. Except for a vague recollection of an

article in *Time,* I was not then acquainted with him or his work. He headed a prominent San Francisco law firm, and I was interested in a job as a lawyer specializing in corporate and securities matters. I vividly remember that first meeting, where I sat spellbound but incredulous as this dynamic man expounded on his ideas. Like the accomplished lawyer he is, he made his case step by step and point by point, with as much conviction and concern for persuasion as if I had been Senator Long.

Although I was receptive to many of his arguments, I rejected his prognostications concerning the economy and the stock market. I had been earning my living as a securities law practitioner and could not conceive of a functional collapse of the public market as a viable source of capital or as a provider of liquidity for shares of public corporations. But this was Kelso's first prediction. He believed that the market was about to commence its biggest tumble in decades and that the Dow was "much more likely to fall to the 600 level than to reach 1,000 in the foreseeable future." Public offerings (up to then my main source of professional income) would virtually cease, Kelso declared with great assurance—as though it had already happened.

After telling me that the casino (his word for "public market apparatus") really is not the best way to finance new capital formation, since it mostly makes the rich richer and does not tend to bring into existence new capital-owning families, he paused. Then, quietly but deliberately, he declared the economy was about to enter a period of unprecedented inflation, with "the dollar worth only a fraction of its present value before the end of the coming decade." As I watched the ships maneuvering in San Francisco Bay, I recall wondering in amused disbelief if this Kelso fellow was really sailing with a full jib. Now, more than 15 years later, I believe that Kelso's prognostications have clearly proved more accurate than those of most of his professional critics.

NOTES

[1] Comptroller General Report to the Senate Finance Committee, "Employee Stock Ownership Plans: Who Benefits Most in Closely Held Companies?" June 20, 1980.

[2] *Harvard Business Review,* November–December 1979.

[3] The name of the corporation has been changed to protect its identity.

Part III
Technical Issues

Chapter 9

Leveraged Buyouts: Legal Problems and Practical Suggestions

H. Bruce Bernstein

Every corporate acquisition presents significant legal questions for the buyer, seller, and—if the acquisition is structured as a leveraged buyout (LBO) financed by a third-party lender—for the lender. These issues are quite numerous and cover a range of subjects too extensive to be adequately addressed in the limited space allotted to this chapter.[1] Therefore this chapter will examine only those questions which are most likely to adversely affect (1) the validity and enforceability of a lender's liens and claims arising in an LBO, and (2) the right of a seller to retain the purchase price received in an LBO and to enforce the claim, if any, the seller may have for the deferred portion of the acquisition price.

Since these issues often directly affect the risk of the lender and the seller, the resolution of these issues will often determine whether an LBO will, in the first instance, be consummated or, if consummated, will result in increased costs to the buyer either in the form of an extra premium paid to the lender or an increased purchase price paid to the seller. These issues also may impact the buyer's potential liability under any guarantees or indemnities which the buyer may have delivered to the seller or lender in connection with the LBO.

The first section of this chapter describes several LBO structures which this author has observed in recent years. Following this section are set forth, in some detail, the principal legal risks faced by lenders

FIGURE 9-1

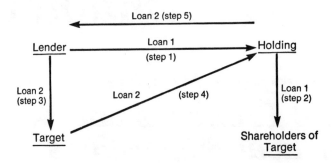

and sellers who participate in LBOs of the types described. The final section briefly summarizes these legal risks and then discusses various procedures and techniques which can be employed in LBOs (1) by lenders, to better ensure the validity and priority of their liens and claims, and (2) by sellers, to better ensure their right to retain the purchase price paid in the LBO and to pursue their claim for any portion of the purchase price remaining unpaid after closing. Since the buyer effectively pays the price for any increased legal risk in an LBO, an understanding of the legal problems present in these transactions may help the buyer minimize the time spent, and thus the expense incurred, in structuring and closing an LBO.

LBO STRUCTURES

LBOs normally involve the purchase of either corporate stock or assets. Stock acquisitions assume many forms, while asset purchases ordinarily involve a single, relatively uncomplicated format.

Stock Acquisitions

Stock Purchases of Subsidiary Corporations. Several forms are illustrated in a series of three figures, with accompanying explanations.

In Figure 9-1, a lender (Lender) makes an unsecured loan to a newly formed holding company (Holding) established for the purpose of entering into a stock purchase agreement with the existing owner(s) (Seller) of the stock of the target company (Target). Proceeds of Lender's initial loan are used by Holding to purchase the stock of Target. Immediately after the closing of the stock purchase, Lender makes a second loan, this time to Target. The proceeds of this second

FIGURE 9–2

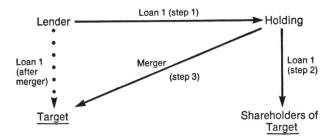

loan are upstreamed to Holding (by dividend, loan, or other distribution), and Holding uses the funds to repay the first loan to Lender. The second loan is secured by liens on the assets of Target.

In Figure 9–2 Lender makes an unsecured loan to Holding, which has been established for the purpose of entering into a stock purchase agreement with Seller. Proceeds of Lender's loan are used by Holding to purchase the stock of Target pursuant to the purchase agreement. Immediately after the stock purchase, Holding is merged downstream into Target. Promptly following the merger, Target (which is the surviving entity in the merger with Holding) grants Lender liens and security interests in and upon Target's assets. It is important to note that in this structure, Lender's loan proceeds are advanced in the first instance to Holding rather than to Target.

In Figure 9–3, pursuant to a stock purchase agreement between Holding and Seller, Holding purchases the stock of Target in exchange for a demand note issued by Holding in favor of Seller. Target thus becomes a wholly owned subsidiary of Holding. Immediately following the stock purchase, Lender makes a secured loan to Target. Target

FIGURE 9–3

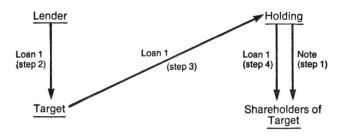

FIGURE 9–4

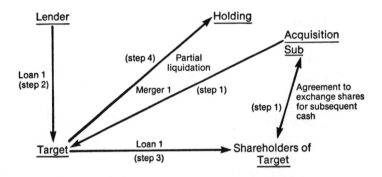

then dividends, lends, or otherwise transfers the loan proceeds to Holding, and Holding in turn uses the proceeds to pay the demand note. This structure enables Lender to advance its loan proceeds directly to Target rather than to Holding. As will be pointed out later in this chapter, it may be very important to Lender that Target, and not some other entity, be the initial recipient of Lender's LBO financing.

Cash Mergers. In a cash merger (see Figure 9–4), an investing group forms Holding, which in turn forms a wholly owned subsidiary (Acquisition Sub). Acquisition Sub and Target enter into a merger agreement, following approval of their respective boards of directors, providing for (1) the merger of Acquisition Sub into Target (Target being the survivor in the merger) and (2) the conversion of the outstanding shares of stock of Target into the right to receive cash at a specified dollar amount per share. (Note that some state business corporation laws *do not permit* cash mergers.) Immediately following the consummation of the merger (which normally will require shareholder approval *before* consummation can occur), Lender makes a secured loan to Target in an amount at least sufficient to enable Target to satisfy its obligations to its "former" shareholders under the merger agreement to exchange their stock for cash. Following the merger, Target becomes a wholly owned subsidiary of Holding; and often, in order to achieve various tax benefits (e.g., a step-up in basis of the Target's fixed assets for future depreciation deductions), the Target will be either wholly or partially liquidated into Holding. This merger technique is often used by investing groups to take publicly held corporations private. It is also used (normally by privately held corporations) to effect what is in reality a stock redemption, when a direct redemption of stock may be prohibited by applicable state redemption statutes.

FIGURE 9–5

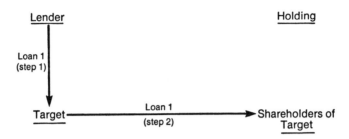

Redemptions. In a typical redemption (illustrated in Figure 9–5), Lender makes a secured loan to Target to enable Target to redeem the stock of one or more of Target's shareholders. While this structure can be used to effect a tender offer by Target of its publicly held stock (assuming compliance with all federal and state tender offer laws, related federal securities acts, and state "blue sky" rules, etc.), the redemption vehicle is most often employed by closely held corporations to purchase the stock of one or more of their shareholders. Following the redemption, the redeemed stock is either held in the corporate treasury or canceled, thereby increasing the percentage of outstanding stock of Target held by each of Target's remaining shareholders.

Tender Offers. Recently this author has witnessed a "leveraged" tender offer structured as follows (see Figure 9–6): The investing group establishes Holding, which in turn forms Acquisition Sub. Acquisition Sub makes a public tender offer for the stock of Target. The

FIGURE 9–6

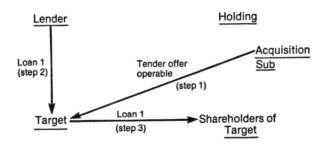

FIGURE 9-7

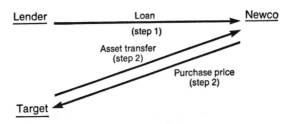

offer provides that the obligation of Acquisition Sub to pay for the tendered stock is conditioned upon (1) the tender of at least 80 percent of Target's stock and (2) the posttender consummation of a cash merger of Target with Acquisition Sub (Target being the survivor).

The tender offer further provides that after the tender offer but *before* Acquisition Sub pays for the tendered shares, Acquisition Sub has the right to vote the tendered shares in favor of the merger. If less than 80 percent of Target's voting stock is tendered or if for any reason the merger of Acquisition Sub into Target is not consummated by a date certain, the shares are required to be returned to the tendering shareholders. This structure enhances the ability of the investing group to "freeze out" the 20 percent minority interest in Target and to permit Lender to determine whether Acquisition Sub's tender offer is successful *before* Lender's loan is made. In this structure Lender does not make its secured loan to Target until *after* the merger takes place.

Asset Acquisitions

Asset acquisitions involving liquidation of Target and a virtually concurrent transfer of the purchase price proceeds to Target's former shareholders may generate legal problems similar to those found in leveraged stock acquisitions.

To illustrate this situation (see Figure 9-7), suppose a new corporation (Newco) is formed to purchase all of the assets and assume substantially all, if not all, of the liabilities of Target. Lender makes a loan to Newco, secured by the assets purchased by Newco from Target. Subject to delays in recordings or registrations of titles, Newco acquires Target's assets (almost) simultaneously with the loan being made by Lender. Promptly following the purchase, Target liquidates, with Lender's loan proceeds being distributed to Target's shareholders. Newco (soon after, or concurrently with, the purchase of Target's assets) changes its name to that formerly used by Target. The substantive result of this transaction is to place Lender's loan proceeds in the hands of Target's former shareholders and to encumber Newco's assets by Lender's liens and security interests. The transaction thus strongly resembles a leveraged stock purchase by Newco, followed by an upstream merger of Target into Newco, and may possibly be so treated for purposes of application of the legal principles discussed in the next section.[2]

If, on the other hand, old Target continues in existence after the asset sale to Newco and does not distribute the asset sales proceeds to the shareholders of old Target, many of the problems associated with leveraged stock acquisitions should not arise. As explained later in this chapter, old Target's unsecured creditors will not be harmed by the asset sale in such circumstances, provided that the price paid by Newco for the assets sold by old Target is either the "present fair salable value" of the assets or a "reasonably equivalent value" for the assets.

The foregoing summary of LBO structures is by no means exhaustive. It is, however, illustrative of several leveraged acquisition techniques this author has observed during the past several years.

APPLICABLE LEGAL AND EQUITABLE PRINCIPLES

The primary focus of this section of this chapter is upon those federal and state laws and equitable principles which are most likely to be employed by a bankruptcy trustee or other third party to attempt to recover the purchase price paid to a seller or set aside and/or subordinate the liens and claims of a lender arising in an LBO. Of greatest importance in this regard are the laws and judicial precedents relating to fraudulent conveyances, bulk transfers, equitable subordination, and corporate distributions.

Fraudulent Conveyances Avoidable under Section 548 of the Code

Under Section 548 of the Federal Bankruptcy Code (the "Code") a debtor-in-possession or trustee (collectively, a trustee), may, under the circumstances described below, avoid any *"transfer* of an interest of the debtor in property, or any *obligation* incurred by the debtor, that was made on or *within one year before the date of the filing* of the [bankruptcy] petition" (emphasis added). There are two general categories of transfers and obligations which can be avoided under Section 548: those that are *actually* fraudulent and those that are *constructively* fraudulent. Transfers or obligations intended "to hinder, delay or defraud creditors" (i.e., transfers fraudulent in fact) are normally accompanied by certain "badges of fraud," several of which may be present in any LBO where the upstreaming of the loan proceeds from the target for the benefit of the target's former shareholders—and to the detriment of the target's then existing and future creditors—renders the target "insolvent" or leaves the target with "an unreasonably small capital" or otherwise unable to pay its debts as they mature.[3]

In order for a transfer or obligation to be *constructively* fraudulent under Section 548, certain elements must be present. First, the transfer must be made or the obligation must be incurred for less than "a reasonably equivalent value."[4] Second, at the time the transfer takes place or the obligation is incurred, or immediately thereafter, (1) the debtor must be "insolvent" or have been rendered "insolvent" by the transfer; *or* (2) the debtor, if engaged in a business, must be left with "an unreasonably small capital;" *or* (3) the debtor must have intended to incur, or believed it would incur, debts that would be beyond its ability to repay. If "reasonably equivalent value" is received by the debtor for a transfer made or obligation incurred, *no* constructive fraudulent conveyance can exist even if, at the time of the transfer or obligation, *all* three of the conditions described above are present. If, however, reasonably equivalent value is not so received, a constructive fraudulent conveyance may exist if *any* one of the three conditions described above is present.

In an LBO, the transfers and obligations that are most susceptible to attack as fraudulent under Section 548 of the Code are:

1. The transfer of purchase price proceeds from the target to the seller in a merger, redemption, or asset acquisition (see, the discussion of those types of acquisitions in the preceding section of this chapter),
2. the transfer of purchase price proceeds from the target to a new holding company in a stock acquisition (see "Stock Acquisitions," above),
3. the transfer by the target to the lender of liens and security interests on the target's assets exchange for the lender's loan to the target,
4. the obligation, if any, of target to seller for the unpaid portion of the stock purchase price, and
5. the obligation of target to lender under the target's loan agreements with lender.

Whether any of the foregoing transfers or obligations are voidable under Section 548 of the Code depends upon (1) the value of the consideration received by the target in exchange for the transfer or obligation and (2) the financial condition of the target immediately following the transfer or obligation. The threshold inquiry in any fraudulent-conveyance analysis is, in other words, what value the debtor received for the transfer made or obligation incurred. The operative words are *value received* by the debtor. As is pointed out later in this chapter, this is quite different from *value paid* by the lender.

From the point of view of the seller, if the LBO is structured as a sale to the target of target stock (whether such sale be outright or pursuant to a cash merger), the seller will be delivering "value" to the target only to the extent of the value to the target of the target stock transferred to it at closing. Normally a corporation's own stock will have no value to the corporation upon the stock's redemption or other direct or indirect (i.e., through the holding company) repurchase, irrespective of whether the stock is canceled or held in the corporation's treasury. Thus, a seller in an LBO which is structured in any of the manners set forth in the first section of this chapter, delivers *no* value in all likelihood (and certainly, therefore, no reasonably equivalent value) to the target in exchange for the purchase price paid directly or indirectly by the target for its own shares. Thus, if *any* of the three general financial condition criteria described in Section 548(a)(2)(B) of the Code is present at the time of the closing of the LBO, the purchase price received by the seller for the target stock *and* the obligation, if any, of the target to pay or fund any deferred portion of the purchase price for its stock, may be subject to avoidance as a fraudulent transfer.

From the point of view of the lender, when the target does not retain the proceeds of the lender's secured loan in the target's business but instead transfers or participates in the transfer of the loan proceeds to the target's then existing or former shareholders, the loan proceeds may not constitute reasonably equivalent value for either (1) the obligation of the target to repay the loan or (2) the liens granted by the target to secure the loan.[5] In any LBO of the type described earlier in this chapter (i.e., a leveraged stock acquisition), the target does not retain the proceeds of the lender's initial advance for use in the target's business but instead transfers these proceeds directly or indirectly to the target's former shareholders in payment for their shares (rather than in payment of a bona fide debt owing by target to these shareholders). Therefore the secured loan results in a dollar-for-dollar reduction in the target's book and real net worth to the extent of the funds paid to the shareholders. Under such circumstances, it is easy to see how a court could conclude that the loan is not reasonably equivalent value for the obligation incurred or for the liens given in exchange for the loan, at least from the point of view of the target's unsecured creditors.[6]

As pointed out above, even if reasonably equivalent value is not delivered by the seller or lender to the target, a constructive fraudulent conveyance under Section 548 of the Code still cannot exist unless one or more of the three conditions described in Section 548(a)(2)(B) is present at the time the transfer is made or the obligation is incurred. Pursuant to the first of these three conditions, if a debtor is or becomes "insolvent" at the time of, or as a result of, a transfer made or obligation incurred for less than a reasonably equivalent value, the transfer and obligation are voidable regardless of the debtor's intent.

"Insolvency" is present when "the sum of [the debtor's] debts is greater than all such [debtor's] property, at a fair valuation, exclusive of [property fraudulently transferred]." (See Code Section 101(29).) Generally stated, "fair valuation" is the "estimate of what can be realized out of the assets within a reasonable time either through collection or sale at the regular market value, conceiving the latter as the amount which could be obtained for the property in question within such period by a 'capable and diligent businessman' from an interested buyer 'who is willing to purchase under ordinary selling conditions.'"[7] This definition is *not* consistent with generally accepted accounting principles (GAAP), and a GAAP balance sheet is therefore irrelevant to a solvency analysis under the Code. With respect to the "debts" half of the insolvency definition, the Code makes it clear that *all* liabilities of the debtor (including contingent, unmatured, and subordinated liabilities) are included in the calculation of debts. Unfunded pension liabilities and outstanding guarantees, for example, are included as liabilities in determining solvency.

In many if not most LBOs, solvency, for purposes of Section 548 of the Bankruptcy Code, is very difficult to determine. Nevertheless, if a seller or lender wishes to be in a position to defend itself adequately in a fraudulent-conveyance action, which defense would in all likelihood (at least for the lender) include an effort to come within the protection of the savings clause of Section 548(c) of the Code (see discussion below), the seller and lender must make a good faith effort to compute, with the help of independent appraisers and auditors, the "fair valuation" of the target's assets and the total amount of the target's debts as of the date on which the LBO takes place. If such a financial analysis demonstrates that the target is or will be rendered insolvent following the acquisition loan and the payment of the purchase price for target's stock, the seller and lender run a substantial risk, if bankruptcy ensues within a year (or possibly much longer than a year) following the LBO,[8] that (1) the seller may have to give back all or a substantial portion of the purchase price received for the target's stock; (2) the lender's liens may be avoided; and (3) the target's post-LBO obligations to the seller and lender may be held unenforceable or subordinated to the claims of the target's other creditors (see discussion of equitable subordination later in this chapter).

Turning to the second condition that can give rise to a constructive fraudulent conveyance, if a debtor engaged in business transfers property or incurs an obligation for less than reasonably equivalent value, the transfer or obligation is fraudulent if it leaves the debtor with "unreasonably small capital," irrespective of the debtor's solvency or intent. Whether the amount of property remaining in the hands of a debtor engaged in business is "unreasonably small" is a question of fact to be determined in each case.[9] Often, a hindsight test is used; namely, if a bankruptcy petition is filed within a year following the transfer (or within the applicable state statute of limitations, if longer),[10] a court could reasonably conclude that the transfer or obligation left the debtor with "unreasonably small capital."[11] Obviously, the less the amount of the lender's loan proceeds transferred to the former shareholders (i.e., the more that is retained in the target's business), the less probable it is that unreasonably small capital will be found to remain after the closing of the LBO.

The above discussion concerning the second of the conditions giving rise to a constructive fraudulent conveyance is equally applicable to the issues presented by the third condition (i.e., intent to incur debts that are beyond the debtor's ability to repay as such debts matured). Further discussion is not, therefore, warranted except to point out that in order to prove the existence of this third condition,

> the trustee must . . . show more than a chronological relation between the act of the debtor and the subsequently incurred debts. Proof must be adduced sufficient to justify the conclusion that the debtor's transfer . . . was contemporaneous with an intent or belief that his subsequent creditors will be injured, *i.e.*, that he will be unable to take care of them as their claims mature. Existence of such a mental attitude on the part of the debtor is inevitably one of fact.[12]

If (1) the transfer of the purchase price proceeds to seller or the transfer of the liens to lender or (2) the incurring of the obligation by the target to the seller to pay any deferred portion of the purchase price or to the lender to repay the loan are "avoided" under Section 548 of the Code, the trustee, under Section 550 of the Code,[13] can recover the property transferred (or, if the court so orders, the value of such property) from the initial transferee of such transfer, or the entity for whose benefit the transfer was made, unless such transferee is able to claim the protection of Section 548(c) of the Code, the section commonly known as the "savings clause."[14]

Under Section 548(c) an initial transferee that gives value to the debtor "in good faith" "has a lien on any interest transferred, may retain any lien transferred, or may enforce any obligation incurred, as the case may be, to the extent that such transferee or obligee gave value to the debtor in exchange for such transfer or obligation." Although "good faith" is not defined in the Code, prior case law has established that good faith "presupposes not only a lack of knowledge of the [transferor's] fraud but also a lack of knowledge of such facts as would put the reasonably prudent person on inquiry. . . . The personal good faith of the [transferee] will not avail him as a defense if he acted with full knowledge of facts and circumstances which put him on inquiry."[15] In any LBO financing, there is probably no more important task for a lender than to attempt to comply *in all respects* with Section 548(c) of the Code.[16]

A seller, on the other hand, may never be able to take advantage of the "saving clause," since the seller arguably gives no "value to the debtor" when it transfers the debtor's stock to the debtor or debtor's parent. The seller would thus be subject to all the trustee's recovery rights under Section 550 of the Code. A sophisticated seller will therefore closely scrutinize the buyer's business plan to determine feasibility, even though the seller may have nothing further owing to it from the buyer after the closing.

For a lender to comply with the savings clause, the lender must (1) give value to the debtor for the obligations incurred and liens granted by the debtor and (2) act at all times "in good faith." Failure to come under the umbrella of Section 548(c) can result in loss of liens *and* loss or subordination of the underlying claims supporting the liens.[17] Such a result would leave the lender in the unenviable position of having to look to third parties involved in the LBO for contribution and indemnity, based upon theories of unjust enrichment and joint tortfeasor liability, in order to recover any portion of its loan. It would also leave any guarantor of the target's liabilities to the lender in a totally exposed position and may lead to the guarantor's personal bankruptcy if its assets are inadequate to cover its obligations.

Fraudulent Conveyances Avoidable under Section 544 of the Code

Under Section 544(b) of the Code, a trustee may use applicable non-bankruptcy law to avoid certain prebankruptcy transfers and obligations. This provision empowers the trustee, among other things, to commence an avoidance action under any applicable state fraudulent-conveyance law. The Uniform Fraudulent Conveyance Act (UFCA), or some variation thereof, is presently in force in 25 states.[18]

In substantially all respects material to the discussion and conclusions contained in this chapter, the UFCA and the provisions of Section 548 of the code are similar. In particular, transfers made and obligations incurred without actual intent to hinder, delay, or defraud present or future creditors can be fraudulent against *present and fu-*

ture creditors of the transferor-obligor under the UFCA only if (1) the transfer is made for less than a fair consideration and (2) the transfer results in the transferor holding, after the transfer, unreasonably small capital or in the transferor intending or believing that it will incur debts beyond its ability to pay as they mature.[19]

A transfer made or an obligation incurred without fair consideration is fraudulent against *present (not future)* creditors under the UFCA only if the transfer is made or obligation is incurred "by a person who is or will be thereby rendered insolvent."[20] Fair consideration is generally defined as "fair equivalent" but requires, in addition, the presence of "good faith."[21] Insolvency exists under the UFCA when "the present fair salable value of [debtor's] assets is less than the amount that will be required to pay his probable liability on his existing debts as they become absolute and matured."[22] The "savings clause" of the UFCA provides, "A purchaser . . . who without actual fraudulent intent has given less than a fair consideration for the conveyance or obligation, may retain the property or obligation as security for repayment.[23]

Probably the most significant difference between Section 548 of the Code and the UFCA is the applicable statute of limitations. As discussed above, transfers completed or obligations incurred more than 12 months prior to bankruptcy cannot be attacked under Section 548 of the Code.[24] Most states which have enacted the UFCA, however, permit fraudulent transfers and obligations to be avoided for several years following their occurrence and/or discovery.[25] While a trustee who relies on state law made applicable by Code Section 544(b) must commence its avoidance action within two years following the trustee's appointment, the trustee may nevertheless rely on the applicable state statute of limitations for fraudulent transfers in order to reach transfers made more than one year prior to the commencement of the bankruptcy case.[26]

Section 544 of the Code and Bulk Sales Laws

In the case of an acquisition involving a sale of assets rather than stock,[27] a trustee for the bankrupt seller may be able to recover the assets sold, through the application of the bulk sales laws of the state in which the transferred assets were located at the time of their transfer.[28]

The essential purpose of the bulk sales laws, now codified in Article 6 of the Uniform Commercial Code (UCC), is to deal with two common types of fraud (which types may also come within the scope of the UFCA):

(a) The merchant, owing debts, who sells out his stock in trade to a friend for less than it is worth, pays his creditors less than he owes them, and hopes to come back into the business through the back door sometime in the near future.

(*b*) The merchant, owing debts, who sells out his stock in trade to anyone for any price, pockets the proceeds, and disappears leaving his creditors unpaid.[29]

Article 6 of the UCC deals with these two situations by requiring that advance notice of the bulk sale be given to the seller's unsecured creditors. Beyond such notice, Article 6 provides little additional protection for the seller's creditors.[30]

Article 6 applies *only* (1) to sellers "whose principal business is the sale of merchandise from stock, including those who manufacture what they sell,"[31] and (2) to transfers "in bulk and not in the ordinary course of the transferor's business of a major part of the materials, supplies, merchandise, or other inventory."[32] Article 6 is thus intended to cover manufacturers, as well as distributors or retailers, but is not intended to include such enterprises as professional service businesses, cleaning businesses, hotels, and restaurants.[33] What constitutes a "major part" of the seller's inventory and whether a major part is to be determined by quantity or value varies from state to state.[34]

If the creditor notice and proceeds distribution requirements of Article 6 are not fulfilled or if the bulk transfer is not otherwise exempt under Section 6–103 from the coverage of the article, the transfer will be "ineffective" against then-existing creditors of the seller. An exemption is generally available if the buyer maintains a known place of business in the same state in which the goods are located prior to their transfer, if the buyer becomes bound to pay the debts of the seller in full and gives public notice of the fact, and if the buyer is solvent after becoming so bound.[35]

If a buyer fails to comply with the notice or exemption provisions of the applicable bulk transfer law, the debtor in possession or trustee of a bankrupt seller may, under code Section 544(b), seek to invalidate the sale and recover the transferred property for the benefit of the seller's creditors. While any such recovery would be subject to a right of setoff in favor of the buyer for the amount of consideration paid for the property transferred,[36] the property recovered would in all likelihood be free of any liens or security interests created by the *buyer*.[37] In order to protect itself against the loss of its liens and security interests in such a situation, a lender should insist on a "bulk sales indemnity" from the seller and should secure the indemnity with a lien, granted by the *seller,* on the assets transferred. Thus, if a trustee for the seller were to obtain a reconveyance of the bulk transfer property, the lender would have its liens in place to secure payment by seller of the amount of damages covered by the seller's indemnity.[38] Here, again, the interests of the guarantor of the target's obligations to the lender and the interests of the lender are identical, since there is less likelihood of the guarantee being enforced if the lender has adequate collateral.

Equitable Subordination

Section 510(c) of the code provides that a bankruptcy court, applying principles of equitable subordination, may subordinate all or part of an allowed claim of a creditor to the allowed claims of any or all other creditors of the debtor or may order any lien securing such a subordinated claim to be transferred to the estate of the debtor. If the transfer of the purchase price proceeds to the seller or the grant to the lender of the liens on the assets of the target are invalidated as fraudulent conveyances in an action where the trustee either has not sought or has not been able to obtain the avoidance of the seller's or lender's claims against the target, the seller and lender will continue to have an allowed claim against the target.[39] The trustee may then seek to invoke the doctrine of equitable subordination to subordinate the seller's and lender's claims to the claims of the other unsecured creditors of the target.

Section 510(c) merely gives statutory sanction to the inherent equitable powers of the bankruptcy court to subordinate claims to prevent unfairness to creditors. Equitable subordination is an extraordinary remedy that is invoked only when a party in a fiduciary relationship with a debtor has engaged in overreaching or fraudulent conduct which has injured the creditors of the debtor.[40] With respect to the conduct of a noninsider creditor, as distinguished from a former shareholder, the standard of misconduct that must be demonstrated to justify equitable subordination is "very substantial."[41]

A lender will be subject to equitable subordination only if (1) it is deemed to have a fiduciary relationship with the target *and* (2) it has engaged in inequitable conduct which has injured the target's other creditors. Generally, a fiduciary relationship will arise where the lender exercises control over the target through such methods as holding a majority of the target's voting stock or managing the target's daily operations.[42] If the fiduciary relationship is present, then an intentional rather than a constructive fraudulent conveyance under Section 548 or 544(b) of the code would in all likelihood constitute conduct sufficiently "inequitable" to permit a bankruptcy court to subordinate the lender's claim against the target to the claims of the target's other creditors.

It should be emphasized that a routine debtor-creditor relationship between lender and target arising out of an LBO financing would not normally give rise to a fiduciary relationship. For example, recommendations by the lender to the target with respect to the target's management, even if accompanied by an implied threat to refuse to extend additional credit if the advice is ignored, does not impose fiduciary duties on the lender.[43] With respect to a seller, however, a fiduciary relationship may be very easy to establish, particularly where the seller held voting control of the target before the LBO.

Restrictions on Corporate Dividends and Other Distributions

In order to protect the rights and interests of unsecured creditors of corporations, states have prohibited corporations from making distributions (by dividend, redemption, or other form of distribution) in amounts that would render the corporations insolvent or otherwise impair the capital of the corporation.[44] Several of the LBO structures delineated in the first section of this chapter call for the target to distribute loan proceeds to a holding company or to the target's shareholders. Although the target may characterize these distributions as loans, the distributions may be held to be dividends or redemptions if there appears to be little likelihood that the loans will or can be repaid to the target.[45] If payment of these dividends or redemptions renders the target insolvent or otherwise impairs its capital in a manner prohibited by state law, the officers and directors authorizing the distributions may be held liable to shareholders or creditors of the target for all payments made in violation of the applicable restrictions.

With respect to corporate distributions made in the context of an LBO, the trustee or other creditors of the target may seek to recover from the seller and/or lender the prohibited distribution on the ground that the seller and lender conspired with the officers and directors of the target to make the illegal distribution. Ordinarily liability for conspiracy arises if two or more parties agree to commit an unlawful act or a lawful act by unlawful means, perform at least one overt act in furtherance of the agreement, and inflict damage on a third party.[46]

It is unclear whether a lender could be held liable for conspiracy because liability for the making of unlawful dividends, redemptions, or other distributions is often statutorily limited to the target's officers and directors who are in a fiduciary relationship with the target. The absence of a fiduciary relationship between lender and target may immunize the lender from any conspiracy liability.

SUMMARY AND CONCLUSIONS

This chapter has attempted to set forth, in some detail, the principal legal risks which face buyers, sellers, and lenders in a typical LBO. While the legal issues and equitable principles discussed herein appear to be complex and confusing, they are in reality simple and straightforward.

The central theme which unifies all of the legal theories discussed above is simply this: Unsecured creditors of an insolvent, cash-poor corporation should be protected from transactions in which the corporation uses the leverage provided by its assets to retire equity *before* debt. Stated in different words, creditors of insolvent corporations are entitled to be paid ahead of the corporations' shareholders. This basic rule of corporate law is embodied in various forms, not the least significant of which are fraudulent conveyance laws, bulk sales laws, equitable subordination principles, state dividend, redemption, and distribution laws, and statutory and common laws concerning the fiduciary responsibility of corporate officers and directors.

The application of some of these laws and principles (principally fraudulent-conveyance laws, bulk sales laws, and equitable subordination) protect unsecured creditors by *invalidating* certain transfers made or obligations incurred by an insolvent or capital-impaired debtor, while the application of the balance of the above-mentioned laws and principles (i.e., state dividend, redemption, and distribution laws, and rules of corporate fiduciary responsibility) protect unsecured creditors by giving them or their representative (i.e., a trustee) a cause of action to recover *damages* from third parties who participated in "unlawful" transfers of the debtor's assets.

Protection from the claims of unsecured creditors and trustees, whether their claims be for avoidance of transfers or obligations or for damages, can best be achieved not through LBO structuring techniques (although some structures are less risk intensive than others) but rather through the selection of targets, and *only* those targets, that can accomplish the proposed LBO without, in the process:

1. Becoming insolvent.
2. Being left with unreasonably small capital.
3. Incurring debts beyond their ability to pay such debts as they mature.
4. Intending to "hinder, delay, or defraud" creditors.
5. Violating applicable state dividend, redemption, or distribution laws or applicable bulk sales laws.

When analyzing a proposed LBO, sellers and lenders should undertake a "good faith" effort to determine whether the target can satisfy the solvency, capital maintenance, cash flow, and asset distribution tests summarized in the preceding paragraph and detailed earlier in this chapter. This effort should then, with the help of counsel, be memorialized in writing and retained with the documents delivered at the closing of the LBO. If the LBO is thereafter attacked by the target's creditors or trustee, much of the evidence necessary to defend or possibly even forestall the threatened litigation will be readily available to the seller and lender, and the difficult and expensive process of reconstructing the target's financial condition as of the closing date will be greatly simplified.

As indicated above, it is imperative that a lender who seeks the sanctuary of the savings clause of the code (i.e., Section 548(c)) be able to sustain the fact that, at the closing of the LBO, when the lender gave "value to the debtor," the lender acted in good faith.[47] Good faith will support a lender's retention of its liens and security interests and its right to enforce its claims against a debtor and the debtor's assets, to the extent of the value given, even if the trustee proves that the debtor's granting of liens and security interests and/or the incurring of obligations was constructively fraudulent. Good faith may also provide a defense against a damage claim for conspiring (1) to effect an "unlawful" dividend, redemption, or other corporate distribution or (2) to aid and abet the breach by a corporate officer or director of its fiduciary duty to the borrower's creditors.

Since a showing of good faith by a lender requires, at a minimum, not only a lack of actual knowledge of the voidability of the transfer or obligation involved but also a "lack of knowledge of such facts as would put a reasonably prudent person or inquiry" of the possible voidability of the relevant transfer or obligation,[48] a prudent lender should conduct a thorough *preclosing* review of the impact of its LBO financing on the existing and future financial condition and projected cash flow of the target. This review should go beyond an analysis of the target's business plan and projections. Investors and principals in LBOs are typically overly optimistic about their ability to "turn around" or better manage the business they are about to own. An LBO is often surrounded by a certain euphoria, prompted by investor excitement and lender anticipation of high closing fees, which can lead borrowers and lenders to accept expectations which, when subjected to more careful review, may be unsupportable. Thus it is the lender's responsibility, for its own protection, to be sure the borrower's data, projections, and appraisals are as accurate, conservative, and reasonable as possible. At a minimum, the lender should make every effort to have its closing file contain as many of the following items as possible:

1. A *pro forma* schedule of assets and liabilities of the borrower, as of the closing date, on a *nonconsolidated* basis, and certified as accurate

by the treasurer or chief financial officer of the borrower. Such schedule should set forth, in footnotes or elsewhere, an explanation of the basis upon which the "fair valuation" or the "present fair salable value" of the borrower's assets was determined.

This schedule should include a list of *all* of the borrower's debts, in the *broadest sense* (including all subordinated debt and such contingent and unmatured liabilities as guaranties, underfunded pension liabilities, projected tort liabilities, and projected contract liabilities), and an explanation of the derivation of the numbers. Of course, the lender's financing must itself be reflected in the schedule as a debt. Particular valuation problems will arise in every transaction, and they should be reviewed with legal and financial experts to confirm that the basis chosen for valuation is reasonable.

2. A conservative cash flow projection for the borrower, on a *nonconsolidated* basis and certified as accurate by the treasurer or chief financial officer of the borrower, covering a period of at least 12 months following the closing date, which projection is based upon historical data (particularly sales levels, costs of goods sold, and employee wage and pension expenses) and not upon what the borrower thinks "it can do for the business" during its first year under new management.

This projection should take into account, if possible, the impact of the LBO and in particular the impact of the separation, if any, of the borrower from its former parent corporation upon the borrower's ability to maintain favorable trade credit terms, supply agreements, unsecured lines of credit, etc. Interest rate assumptions will, of course, be critically important. The projections should also, if possible, demonstrate that the borrower's cash needs during the relevant 12-month period will be met either by internally generated funds or by loan availability under the lender's secured line of credit.

3. A certificate from the treasurer or chief financial officer of the borrower, stating that all payables, other than those being disputed (while adequately reserved for), are current and not past due.

4. A letter from the borrower's outside auditors stating that during the course of the auditors' most recent audit of the borrower and during the course of the auditors' preclosing review of the unaudited financial statements of the borrower, nothing came to the attention of the auditors which caused them to believe that the borrower was not solvent as warranted by borrower in the loan agreements between borrower and lender. These letters are often difficult to obtain and may not add significantly to the information described in paragraphs 1–3 above. Moreover, an attempt to obtain such letters which fails may be harmful.

5. A legal opinion from borrower's counsel (preferably independent, outside counsel), based upon the same facts and financial information

as is available to lender, opining among other things (1) that the transfer of funds from the lender to the borrower and thereafter to the borrower's former shareholders complies with applicable state corporate laws and judicial precedents and does not result in an "unlawful" dividend, redemption, or other distribution; and (2) that all preclosing mergers, if any, required as part of the LBO structure have been duly and validly consummated and are enforceable and effective under applicable law.

6. In an asset sale, evidence of compliance with, or exemption from, applicable state bulk sales laws. Exemption under UCC Section 6-103 may require the publication, in one or more newspapers of general circulation where the seller maintains its principal place of business, of notice which includes the names and addresses of the buyer and seller and the effective date of the proposed transfer. The evidence needed to prove compliance with the creditor notice and payment application provisions of Article 6 of the UCC will vary from state to state depending upon the requirements of the local statute. If bulk sales compliance is not possible, the lender should obtain an indemnification from the seller and secure payment of the indemnity with a lien on the assets transferred. (See discussion of bulk sales laws in the preceding section of this chapter.)

7. An acknowledgment, signed by the seller, confirming that the seller is aware that it is participating in a leveraged acquisition. If the loan transaction and the stock or asset purchase are collapsed and treated as a single, integrated transaction, this acknowledgment may be important to ensuring that ultimate liability for any fraudulent transfer or other proscribed transaction comes to rest on the seller, the real beneficiary of the LBO, rather than the lender.

These items are admittedly difficult, and often costly, to obtain. Failure to properly assemble them, however, can significantly impact the level of risk to the seller, the lender, and the buyer—not only in terms of the ultimate disposition of the case but in terms of the cost and time commitment involved in extensive litigation.

The structure of an LBO ultimately selected by the seller and lender in order to minimize their respective legal risks will depend upon various factors, including (1) the ability of the target, under applicable state law, to effect any dividend, redemption, or other distribution required to satisfy the stock purchase obligation of the holding company (e.g., a cash merger may be possible when a redemption is not); (2) the preservation or generation of certain tax advantages for the borrower (e.g., a cash merger followed by a partial liquidation may yield a step-up in the basis of depreciable property not possible following a redemption or tender offer); (3) the maintenance of favorable leases, supply contracts, low-coupon debentures, and other agreements (which would terminate or necessitate expensive third-party consents if assets, rather than stock of the borrower, were sold).

Notwithstanding all of these factors, which will vary from transaction to transaction, an LBO structure should be utilized in *every* transaction which results in the lender making its loan to the target or to the entity that is buying the target's assets (i.e., the lender must give its value "to the debtor") and in the selling obtaining a purchase price package (i.e., possibly including nonvoting preferred stock, rather than subordinated debt) which leaves the post-LBO target solvent and able to pay its debts for the foreseeable future.

NOTES

1. These "other issues" arise from the application, in the LBO context, of a number of laws, including (1) federal antitrust, tax, labor, ERISA, and environmental laws; (2) federal and state securities laws and related proxy, registration, antifraud, takeover, and tender offer rules; and (3) state laws concerning shareholder dissenters' rights and products liability. While these issues are very significant to the successful closing and subsequent performance of most LBOs and are potentially loss generating for a seller or lender, they are not treated in this chapter.

2. See *Grant-Howard Associates* v. *General Housewares Corp.*, 454 N.Y.S.2d 521 (1982), *aff'd,* 467 N.Y.S.2d 1018 (1st Dept. 1983), where a purchaser of assets was held liable for injuries caused by products manufactured and sold by the seller even though the purchase agreement limited such liability to obligations which existed as of the date the purchase transaction was closed. In this case, the court noted, at 524, that "[the] characterization of the acquisition by the parties is not the controlling factor. It is the terms, substance and legal effect of the agreement which should be considered." The court focused on the continuity of management, personnel, physical location, assets, and general business operations between the selling and purchasing corporation and ruled that since the purchaser received the advantage of a going concern, it should bear the costs associated with that benefit. The author believes that the rationale of *Grant-Howard* could logically be extended to an asset acquisition substantially similar to that described in this section of the chapter.

3. See §548(a) which provides:

> The trustee may avoid any transfer of an interest of the debtor in property, or any obligation incurred by the debtor, that was made or incurred on or within one year before the date of the filing of the petition, if the debtor—
> 1. Made such transfer or incurred such obligation with actual intent to hinder, delay, or defraud any entity to which the debtor was or became, on or after the date that such transfer occurred or such obligation was incurred, indebted; or
> 2. A. Received less than a reasonably equivalent value in exchange for such transfer or obligation; and
>   B. (i) Was insolvent on the date that such transfer was made or such obligation was incurred, or became insolvent as a result of such transfer or obligation;
>   (ii) Was engaged in business, or was about to engage in business or a transaction, for which any property remaining with the debtor was an unreasonably small capital; or
>   (iii) Intended to incur, or believed that the debtor would incur, debts that would be beyond the debtor's ability to pay as such debts matured.

See, generally, Cook, "Fraudulent Transfer Liability under the Bankruptcy Code," 17 *Houston L. Rev.* 263, 270–276 (1980) (and cases cited and discussed therein relating to §548(a)(1) and its predecessor section under the former Bankruptcy Act, §67d(2)(d)). Also see, e.g., *U.S.* v. *Gleneagles Investment Co., Inc.,* 565 F. Supp. 556 (M.D. Pa. 1983) (where the court applied the intentional fraud provisions of Pennsylvania's Uniform Fraudulent Conveyance Act in a case where a lender was found to have known the adverse impact of the LBO on the target's unsecured creditors).

4. See §548(a)(2)(A). "Reasonably equivalent value" replaced the former Bankruptcy Act's "fair consideration" standard as the essential condition precedent to a constructive fraudulent conveyance. See §67d(1)(e) of the Bankruptcy Act. The "fair consideration" standard may, however, be applicable under §544(b) of the code to the "transfer" of liens to the lender in an LBO financing. (See discussion of the Uniform Fraudulent Convey-ance Act in section on fraudulent conveyances below.)

5. See *U.S.* v. *Gleneagles Investment Co.* (Note 3, above) at pp. 574–575; cf., *In re Venie,* 80 F. Supp. 250 (W.D.Mo. 1948); *Edward Hines Western Pine Co.* v. *First National Bank of Chicago,* 61 F.2d 503 (7th Cir. 1932); *Bullard* v. *Aluminum Company of America,* 468 F.2d 11 (7th Cir. 1972). But see *In re Greenbrook Carpet Co., Inc.,* 722 F.2d 659 (11th Cir. 1984), where the court refused to collapse the loan transaction into the stock purchase and held that the lender's loan proceeds constituted "reasonably equivalent value" under §548 of the code for the security interest granted the lender, notwithstanding the fact that the debtor did not utilize the proceeds in the debtor's business.

6. See *U.S.* v. *Gleneagles Investment Co.* (above, Note 3).

7. 2 *Collier on Bankruptcy,* ¶101.26 at 101-57–101-58 (15th ed. 1983). At 101-60–101-61, Collier points out:

> Real estate and other tangible fixed assets have been appraised at their fair selling price by consideration of a variety of factors. Ordinarily the issue calls for expert opinion, but such judgment may be formed on the basis of widely varying elements covering not only physical characteristics such as location, type of business for which the premises are designed or suited, or age and condition, but also original costs and past and prospective earnings or other pertinent factors.

Accounts receivable, according to Collier (at 101-58–101-59) are to be "appraised on the basis of the prospect, at the critical date, of their collectibility within a reasonable time, depending on the solvency of the obligor the presence or absence of a serious dispute over their validity or the availability of other defenses." Inventory is "to be valued with due regard for the age and condition of the stock, the season of the year, and the general state of the trade." One court has construed the analogous "fair consideration" requirement of the Bankruptcy Act to mean, with respect to real property, at least 70 percent of fair market value. See *Durrett* v. *Washington National Insurance Co.,* 621 F.2d 201, 203 (5th Cir. 1980). For other cases using a *Durrett* approach, see *In re Richardson,* 23 B.R. 434 (Bankr. D. Utah 1982); *In re Gilmore,* 31 B.R. 615 (E.D. Wash. 1983); *In re Richard,* 26 B.R. 560 (Bankr. D.R.I. 1983); *In re Smith,* 21 B.R. 345 (Bankr. N.D. Fla. 1982); *In re Bates,* 32 B.R. 40 (Bankr. E.D. Cal. 1983); *In re Ewing,* CCH Bankr. L. Reptr. ¶69,460 (Bankr. W.D. Pa. 1983).

8. See discussion in Fraudulent Conveyances below of state statutes of limitation applicable under the Uniform Fraudulent Conveyance Act.

9. 4 *Collier on Bankruptcy,* ¶548.04 at 548-48 (15th ed. 1983).

10. See, e.g., Cal. C.P.C. §338–4 (three years); Texas Civ. Stat. Art. 5529 (four years); New York CPLR §213 subd. 1 (six years); see also *In re Bethune,* 8 B.R. 1101 (Bankr. N.D. Ala. 1982).

11. See, e.g., *In re Desert View Building Supplies, Inc.* (D. Nev. No. BK-LV-76-785, opinion dated August 16, 1977), *aff'd sub nom Wells Fargo Bank* v. *Desert View Building Supplies,* 475 F. Supp. 693 (D. Nev. 1978), *aff'd without opinion,* 633 F.2d. 225 (9th Cir. 1980).

12. 4 *Collier on Bankruptcy,* ¶548.05 at 548-50–548-51 (15th ed. 1983); also see *U.S.* v. *Gleneagles Investment Co.* (above, Note 3).

13. See 124 Cong. Rec. H11,097 (Sept. 28, 1978); S17,414 (Oct. 6, 1978): "This means that liability is not imposed on a transferee to the extent that the transferee is protected under a provision such as Section 548(c) which grants a good faith transferee for value of a transfer that is avoided only as a fraudulent transfer, a lien on the property transferred to the extent of value given." (Note: §550 contains its own statute of limitations; see §550(e).)

14. See Cook (above, Note 2), at 283.

15. *Chorost* v. *Grand Rapids Factory Showrooms, Inc.,* 77 F. Supp. 276, 281 (D.N.J.), *aff'd,* 172 F.2d 327 (3d Cir. 1949); also see 4 *Collier on Bankruptcy* ¶548.07 (15th ed. 1982); *In re Peoria Braumeister Co.,* 138 F.2d 520 (7th Cir. 1943); cf., *U.S.* v. *Gleneagles Investment Co.* (above, Note 3). Also see Note, "Good Faith and Fraudulent Conveyances," 97 Harv. L. Rev. 495 (1983).

16. This effort becomes doubly important in connection with LBOs involving assets located in states which have adopted the UFCA, which contains its own "savings clause." See discussion of the UFCA in "Fraudulent Conveyances" below.

17. Cf., *U.S.* v. *Gleneagles Investment Co.* (Note 3, above). *Gleneagles* expressly deals with the question, in an LBO setting, of whether a lender who receives both a fraudulent obligation (i.e., claim) and a fraudulent conveyance can assert the avoided obligation as an unsecured claim in the case, subject to the court's equitable power to subordinate the claim. In the case of *In re Desert View Building Supplies, Inc.* (Note 11, above), the lender's lien was avoided under the Nevada Uniform Fraudulent Conveyance Act, but the lender's resulting unsecured claim was left intact because avoidance was based on the section of the Uniform Fraudulent Conveyance Act which is limited to "conveyance(s) made" rather than "obligation(s) incurred." (See Uniform Fraudulent Conveyance Act §5.) Also, in *Desert View,* since the relevant conveyance took place more than 12 months before bankruptcy, Section 67d of the Bankruptcy Act was unavailable to the trustee. There was some indication in the bankruptcy judge's original opinion in *Desert View,* however, that the lender's claim, if it had been found to be a fraudulent obligation, would have been subordinated, not invalidated. In the case of *In re Process-Manz Press, Inc.,* 236 F. Supp. 333 (N.D. Ill. 1964), *rev'd on jurisdictional grounds,* 369 F.2d 513 (7th Cir. 1966), *cert. denied,* 386 U.S. 957 (1967), the lender's liens were avoided and its claims subordinated under circumstances where the issue of avoidability of the lender's claims was not presented. Research has confirmed that a finding that a transferee has participated in an intentional fraudulent conveyance may well provide the basis for invalidation of the underlying obligation as well as the security for its repayment. See e.g., 4 *Collier on Bankruptcy,* ¶67.41, p. 597 (14th ed. 1975); 4 *Collier on Bankruptcy,* ¶548.07 at pp. 548-68–548-70 (15th ed. 1983); *McWilliams* v. *Edmonson,* 162 F.2d 454, 456-57 (5th Cir. 1947), *cert. denied,* 332 U.S. 835 (1947); *Lowenstein* v. *Reikes,* 60 F.2d 933,936 (2d Cir. 1932), *cert. denied,* 287 U.S. 669 (1932); *In re Spotless Tavern Co.,* 4 F. Supp. 752, 755 (D. Md. 1933); *Potter* v. *Walker,* 2 F.2d 774, 778 (E.D.N.Y. 1924), *aff'd,* 2 F.2d 1020 (2d Cir. 1924); *In re Friedman,* 164 F. 131, 143 (E.D. Wisc. 1908); *In re Hugill,* 100 F. 616, 618 (N.D. Ohio 1900); *Goll* v. *Stefanski,* 108 A. 189, 190 (N.J. App. 1919).

There are cases that find a distinction between actual fraud and the mere absence of the kind of good faith that would allow the lender to take advantage of the savings clause to retain a lien for repayment of money advanced. See, e.g., *In re Allied Development Corp.*, 435 F.2d 372, 376 (7th Cir. 1970). In *Allied,* a bank which was found not to have participated in an actual fraud but still not to be in good faith, was *not* allowed to take advantage of the savings clause of §67(d)(6) to retain a lien on the property in question to secure repayment of its obligation, but it was allowed to retain its obligation. The risk that the lender will be deemed to have participated in an intentional fraud has been increased by *Gleneagles* and decisions construing §548(a)(1) and the code such as *In re American Properties, Inc.,* 14 B.R. 637, 642-43 (Bankr. D. Kan. 1981), and *In re Health Gourmet, Inc.,* 29 B.R. 673, 676 (Bankr. D. Mass. 1983).

18. See 4 *Collier on Bankruptcy* ¶544.02 at p. 544-12 (15th ed. 1983) (regarding the location of debtor or location of collateral as determinant of which state's fraudulent transfer law is applicable).

19. See UFCA §§5 and 6. (But note that §5 applies only to "transfers made," not "obligations incurred.")

20. See UFCA §4.

21. See UFCA §3(a). The "good faith" element has been dropped from the "reasonably equivalent value" standard contained in §548 of the code. The presence of the "good faith" requirement in UFCA §3(a) may require the lender to do even more "homework" before closing an LBO financing. See *U.S.* v. *Gleneagles Investment Co.* at 574.

22. See UFCA §2(1). Because debts can be reduced to reflect a debtor's "probable liability" thereon, solvency may be easier to prove under the UFCA than under §101(26) of the code. "Present fair salable value" and "fair valuation," as tests for valuing a debtor's assets, are in all likelihood interchangeable. See Cook (above, Note 2), at 277. *But see U.S.* v. *Gleneagles Investment Co.* (above, Note 3), which suggests that "*present* fair salable value*" (emphasis added) may be closer to liquidation value.

23. See UFCA §9(2). Since "fair consideration" includes the element of "good faith", the principal difference between §9(2) of the UFCA and §548(c) of the code is the requirement that the transferee be "without actual fraudulent intent." Based upon a review of the cases and commentaries dealing with the requirement of the absence of "actual fraudulent intent," the author does not believe this requirement to be particularly significant to the discussion contained in this chapter or to the conclusions otherwise expressed herein. See 4 *Collier on Bankruptcy* ¶548.07 at 548-68 and 548-69 (15th ed. 1983); cf., *McWilliams* v. *Edmonson,* 162 F.2d 454 (5th Cir. 1947), *cert. denied,* 332 U.S. 835 (1947) (where the court seems to treat good faith and the absence of fraudulent intent as interchangeable expressions). But see *In re Allied Development Corp.,* 435 F.2d 372 (7th Cir. 1970) (where the court distinguishes good faith from absence of fraudulent intent).

24. See §548(d)(1), which sets forth *when* a transfer is deemed to have taken place. The trustee must file its avoiding action under §548 within two years of his appointment. See §546(a) of the code. If a trustee is never appointed in the case, there would appear to be no limitation, except the closing or dismissal of the case, on the time within which the avoidance action must be brought.

25. See Note 10 above.

26. An argument was made in *Gleneagles* (above, Note 3), at 583, that the Pennsylva-

nia statute of limitations was not binding on a trustee if *any actual creditor* of the bankrupt, such as the United States, was not subject to the state statute of limitations. If this argument is correct, there is no cutoff of the UFCA risk for a lender or seller whenever the United States is a creditor, as it usually is.

27. See Asset Acquisitions in this chapter.

28. Uniform Commercial Code (1980 ed.) (UCC) §6-102(4) "[A]ll bulk transfers of goods located within this state are subject to this Article."

29. UCC §6-101, Official Comment 2.

30. Some states have, however, adopted UCC §6-106, an optional provision which requires the buyer to hold the sales proceeds for the seller's creditors until their claims are satisfied. This provision has not been widely adopted.

31. UCC §6-102(3).

32. UCC §6-102(1).

33. UCC §6-102, Official Comment 2.

34. See Coogan, Hogan, and Vagts, *Secured Transactions under the UCC* §22.06[1][a], [b], and [c] (1981); Rapson, "Article 6 of the Uniform Commercial Code: Problems and Pitfalls in Conducting Bulk Sales," 68 *Com. L.J.* 226 (1963).

35. UCC §6-103(6). See UCC §6-103 for a list of other exemptions from Article 6.

36. See *In re Verco Industries*, 704 F.2d 1134 (9th Cir. 1983).

37. If the sale to the buyer was "ineffective," a persuasive argument could be made by the trustee that the buyer never acquired sufficient rights in the property transferred to permit a lien thereon or security interest therein to attach to such property.

38. Query: Could the lien securing seller's indemnity be voided as a matter of public policy? The answer to this question may depend upon the lender's involvement in the transfer and whether the transfer also constituted an intentional fraudulent conveyance under the UFCA.

39. See Note 17, above.

40. *In re W. T. Grant,* 4 B.R. 53, 74–75 (Bankr. S.D.N.Y. 1980).

41. *In re W. T. Grant* (above, Note 40), at 75. For a general explanation of doctrine of equitable subordination, see Herzog & Zweibel, "The Equitable Subordination of Claims in Bankruptcy," 17 *Vand. L.Rev.* 83 (1961); *In re Mobile Steel Company,* 563 F.2d 692,700 (5th Cir. 1977); *In re Bowman Hardware & Electric Co.,* 67 F.2d 792, 794 (7th Cir. 1933); *In re Prima Co.,* 98 F.2d 952 (7th Cir. 1938), *cert. denied,* 305 U.S. 658 (1938); *Farmers Bank of Clinton* v. *Julian,* 383 F.2d 314 (8th Cir. 1967), *cert. denied* 389 U.S. 1021 (1967).

42. *In re American Lumber Company,* 5 B.R. 470 (D. Minn. 1980); *In re Process-Manz Press, Inc.* (above, Note 17).

43. *In re W. T. Grant Co.*, 699 F.2d 599, 610 (2nd Cir. 1983), *cert. denied,* 104 S.Ct. 89 (1983).

44. See, e.g., Delaware Corporation Law §170; Illinois Business Corporation Act §41.

45. *U.S.* v. *Gleneagles Investment Co.* (above, Note 3), at 584-5.

46. *Lenard* v. *Argento,* 699 F.2d 874, 882 (7th Cir. 1983), *cert. denied,* 104 S.Ct. 69 (1983).

47. Note discussion in the second section of this chapter regarding the probable un-availability to sellers of §548(c) of the code because of the absence of any "value" delivered to the target in exchange for the stock or assets transferred. (See Asset Acquisitions.)

48. See Note 15, above.

Chapter 10

Tax and Accounting Considerations

Joseph A. Kitzes
Donald H. Lamb

Previous chapters have highlighted the conflicting pressures imposed on an LBO structure by the differing needs of the buyer, the seller, and the financiers. Some of these impact structure, while others impact price. The tax and accounting aspects of a transaction can impact both. Too often we have seen a deal fail at the wire because these critical aspects weren't adequately planned up front.

This chapter will highlight the various matters that you should consider with your tax and accounting advisers when analyzing a leveraged buyout transaction. Because there are many, sometimes conflicting, objectives involved, the tax aspects of LBOs require careful study and analysis. It is the accountant's job to assist his clients in preparing an analysis of the financial impact of the various alternatives available in structuring an LBO. In addition, once a tentative agreement is reached, the accountant should perform an acquisition audit of the buyout candidate.

The following definitions will be used in the "tax considerations" portion of this chapter:

A is the corporate vehicle, generally a newly formed corporation, used to acquire the target corporation.

S is a wholly owned subsidiary of A that may be formed by A for purposes of the acquisition.

T is the target, or to-be-acquired, corporation.

M is the existing management of T. M often participates in A's leveraged buyout of T.

TAX CONSIDERATIONS

Although more complex forms can be adopted to meet the needs of a particular situation, most midsized acquisitions are structured either as a purchase of all of T's stock or all of T's assets.

Purchase of Stock

In general, if the purchase price is less than the book value of T's assets, the tax advantages of a stock buyout outweigh the tax advantages of an asset purchase. Even in those transactions where the purchase price exceeds the book value of the assets, a stock buyout may be preferred if T has a large net operating loss carryover, since the buyers of T could normally continue to use T's net operating loss carryovers. As is discussed in previous chapters, however, the tax aspect is only one of many variables that affect the structure of the LBO and may not, in itself, control the structure.

Structuring the Acquisition. In the simplest type of stock buyout, M arranges financing to permit A to acquire the stock of T directly from T's shareholders. In instances where T may have too many shareholders for A to deal with each directly or where T has some shareholders that are reluctant (for one reason or another) to accept A's offer, A can form S to acquire T's controlling shares and subsequently merge S into T. This merger will achieve the same tax results as a purchase of T's stock by A. The tax treatment of this type of transaction will depend on the source of the consideration given to T's shareholders.

Tax Treatment of T's Shareholders. If T's shareholders receive cash or notes from T, S will be regarded as transitory, and the merger will be treated as a redemption by T of its stock. Similarly, if T's shareholders receive cash or notes from A, S will be regarded as transitory, and the merger will be treated as a purchase by A of T's stock. If notes are received from either T or A, T's shareholders will generally be able to use the installment method of income reporting. This method allows the selling shareholders to report only a part of their total gain on the sale each time they collect a part of the purchase price for their stock. An exception to applicability of the installment method would occur if the redemption is deemed to be essentially equivalent to a dividend. The use of A stock to compensate T's shareholders will cause T's shareholders to be taxed on the fair market value of the A stock received.

Each of T's shareholders would qualify for capital gain treatment on the sale of his stock. The holding period necessary to obtain *long-term* capital gain treatment is currently 12 months and a day for stock acquired on or before June 22, 1984. In the case of stock acquired after June 22, 1984, and before January 1, 1988, the holding period for long-term capital gain and loss treatment is reduced from "more than one year" to "more than six months." For noncorporate shareholders, the maximum effective tax rate on a long-term capital gain is 20 percent. The noncorporate shareholder's tax adviser should determine whether or not the alternative minimum tax is applicable. There is a 28 percent tax rate on long-term capital gains by corporations and there is also the possibility that a corporation may be subject to the add-on minimum tax.

The Section 338 Election

Frequently A will acquire the stock of T with the objective of acquiring T's assets. This would be the case when the fair market value of T's assets, as reflected in the purchase price of the stock, exceeded T's basis in its assets. The rules that govern the treatment of a stock purchase as a direct purchase of T's assets were changed substantially by the addition of a new Section 338 and the amendment of Section 334(b)(2) as part of the Tax Equity and Fiscal Responsibility Act of 1982 (TEFRA).

Making the Election. Under the new rules, A can treat the acquisition of T's stock as an asset acquisition by making an election not later than (1) 75 days after the acquisition date or (2) the 60th day after the date the IRS publishes the first set of temporary regulations after the temporary regulations it published in Treasury Decision 7942 on February 8, 1984, whichever comes earlier.

The Tax Reform Act of 1984 (TRA) changes the period in which the above election can be made retroactively to September 1, 1982. Under TRA, the election can be made up to the 15th day of the ninth month following the month in which the requisite 80 percent control is acquired. However, regulations can provide for other election dates. In addition, any election as to a qualified stock purchase made before September 1, 1982, can be made up to September 16, 1984.

In order to make a Section 338 election, A must make a "qualified stock purchase" in T. A qualified stock purchase is any transaction or series of transactions in which, during a 12-month period, A purchases (1) T stock possessing at least 80 percent of T's total voting power and (2) at least 80 percent of the shares of each class of T's nonvoting stock (except stock which is limited and preferred as to dividends). The acquisition date is the date on which A first meets these requirements. Therefore, if A purchases 50 percent of T's stock on January 1, 20 percent on March 1, and 30 percent on April 1 of the same year, the acquisition date is April 1.

"Deemed Sale" of Assets. If A makes a Section 338 election, T is treated as having adopted a plan of liquidation and having sold all of its assets to a new corporation (New T) at the close of the acquisition date in a single transaction to which Section 337 applies. This is a significant change from the prior rules. T does not actually have to liquidate in order to be treated as having adopted a plan of liquidation. This rule is especially helpful in those situations where the transfer of T's assets would require the consent of third parties.

Under the general rule of Section 337, no gain or loss is recognized on the sale of property as part of a complete liquidation, so that the deemed sale is tax free. Section 337 is limited to A's percentage ownership of T's stock. For example, if A makes a Section 338 election after purchasing 80 percent of T's stock, T must pay tax on 20 percent of its gain on the deemed sale of its assets.

The above limitation on the nonrecognition of gain or loss is imposed in lieu of a tax on minority shareholders who do not sell their stock. For this reason, the tax on the target company is often referred to as the "surrogate tax." TRA imposes several restrictions that are designed to limit the nonrecognition of gain or loss by a target corporation in situations involving the so-called surrogate tax. These restrictions generally limit nonrecognition treatment for transactions that occur after the acquisition date to situations in which stock held by minority shareholders is disposed of in taxable transactions.

Applicability of Various Recapture Provisions. The deemed sale of T's assets under Section 337 triggers various types of recapture and other tax considerations, including investment tax credit (ITC), depreciation, last-in first-out (LIFO) inventory reserve, tax benefit (expense), and domestic international sales corporation (DISC) income, along with gain on appreciated stock in certain types of foreign corporations. These recapture items must be reported on the final tax return of T. This is because the deemed sale and liquidation under Section 337 occurs at the close of the acquisition date, and the purchase by New T occurs as of the beginning of the day after the acquisition date. Net operating losses and all other tax attributes of T are extinguished with the final return.

One factor that A should consider in a Section 338 transaction is the potential for inheriting a tax liability caused by the deemed sale of the assets of T. As a result of this potential liability, tax reimbursement agreements are often drafted as part of the transaction in order to compensate the buyer for any tax liability assumed.

Final Tax Return of T. T's final return is due on the 15th day of the third month following the month in which the acquisition date occurs. If T is the common parent of an affiliated group filing a consolidated return, the recapture items would be reported in a final consolidated return of T's group. When T is a member of an affiliated group filing a consolidated return prior to the acquisition, the recapture items will not be included in the consolidated return of the selling group. T is required to file a separate one-day "deemed sale return" that includes the recapture items. T's tax attributes can be used in the return.

The regulations provided a special election that permits T's recapture items to be included in the consolidated return of the selling group. The tax attributes of the selling group can then be used to shelter T's recapture items. Under this election, the deemed sale of assets is treated as a taxable sale of assets by T. Gain or loss recognized by T is then reported in the selling group's consolidated return. No gain or loss is recognized on the stock actually sold by the selling group.

Computation of Selling Price. T's assets are treated as sold to New T for an amount generally equal to A's "grossed-up" basis in T's stock, adjusted for T's liabilities and other relevant factors. For example, if A purchased all of T's stock for $1,000 and T had liabilities of $200, New T's basis for its assets would be $1,200.

If less than 100 percent of the stock of T is acquired, the grossed-up basis is defined as an amount equal to A's basis in its T stock multiplied by a fraction. The numerator of this fraction is 100 percent, and the denominator is the percentage of stock (by value) of T held by A on the acquisition date. For example, assume A purchased 900 of T's 1,000 shares for $900 and made an election under Section 338. The grossed-up basis to be allocated to T's assets would be $1,000, determined as follows:

$$\$900 \times \$100 \div \$90 = \$1,000.$$

TRA contains changes to the "deemed sales" and the "deemed purchase" rules as originally enacted by TEFRA. It almost totally revised the grossed-basis rules illustrated above.

Under TRA, the deemed sales price of T's assets is the fair market value of old T's assets at the acquisition date. In addition, the fair market value can be determined on the basis of a formula contained in regulations which take into account liabilities, including recapture taxes, and other relevant items. These regulations may also permit the use of competent appraisals to establish fair market value for the assets in those cases where the formula method is not selected by the taxpayer.

TRA provides a new method for determining the deemed purchase price. The deemed purchase price that is used in determining the basis of T's assets is the grossed-up basis of T's stock that is purchased by the acquiring corporation during so much of the acquisition period that ends on the acquisition date plus its basis in other target stock that it owns on the acquisition date. Such acquisitions are called "recently purchased stock" and "nonrecently purchased stock," respectively. Adjustments are then to be made for the target's liabilities, including any recapture taxes, and other relevant items.

Consistency Provisions. Two provisions in Section 338 are designed to prevent A from selectively stepping up the basis of some assets. If A or an A affiliate makes a qualified stock purchase in T and one or more T affiliates during the "consistency period," a Section 338 election made with respect to T will also apply to T affiliates. If an election is not made for T, A cannot make an election for a T affiliate. Generally, the consistency period begins one year before the first T stock purchase included in a qualified stock purchase and ends one year after the acquisition date. Since the stock acquisition period may be up to a 12-month period, the consistency period may be as long as three years.

The second consistency provision is designed to prevent A from purchasing some assets directly from T and acquiring the remaining assets through a stock acquisition. If A purchases any asset of T or a T affiliate during the consistency period, the corporation will be treated as having made an election under Section 338.

These two consistency provisions are illustrated by the following two examples.

Example 1. A makes a qualified stock purchase of T's stock. The acquisition date is January 1, 1984. A makes a timely Section 338 election. A also makes a qualified stock purchase of T_2, an affiliate of T. The acquisition date is June 1, 1984, and A does not make a Section 338 election with respect to the purchase of T_2's stock. Nevertheless, an election is deemed made, since a qualified purchase of T_2's stock was completed less than a year after the acquisition date with respect to T, and the election was made with respect to T.

Example 2. A buys the assets of S_1 and S_2. Both are wholly owned subsidiaries of T. A's purchase of S_1's assets mandates a Section 338 election with respect to A's purchase of S_2's stock.

There are some exceptions to the deemed election rule. If any of the following applies, the acquisition of the asset will not trigger a Section 338 election:

1. If the sale of the asset occurs in the ordinary course of business.
2. If the asset is acquired with a carryover basis.
3. If the asset was acquired before September 1, 1984.
4. If the property is located outside the United States and is described in regulations to be issued.

The consistency provisions are broad in scope, and their application is mandatory. Careful planning is required to ensure that a prohibited asset acquisition does not occur during the consistency period if A does not intend to make a Section 338 election.

Tax Treatment if a Section 338 Election Is Not Made

It was earlier discussed that by making an election under Section 338, all the tax attributes of T would be eliminated. Let's now assume that A purchases all of T's stock, does not make a Section 338 election, and then immediately merges T upstream into A or liquidates T into A. The result is that T's tax attributes (including net operating losses) carry over to A. A would receive and be able to use the carryovers of T following its liquidation.

This possibility was considered by many to be a TEFRA-created loophole. Substantial technical corrections were proposed to Section 338 late in 1983 in HR 4170. One of those proposed corrections would have provided for the disallowance of carryovers and other tax benefits received by a parent in a liquidation if a subsidiary was previously acquired in a qualified stock purchase. This proposed rule would only apply when the principal purpose of the liquidation was the evasion or avoidance of federal income tax through the use of these tax attributes that the parent corporation would not otherwise enjoy.

TRA did provide an explicit rule that permits the IRS to disallow deductions, carryovers, credits, and other items upon the liquidation of a corporation that has been acquired by means of a qualified stock purchase. This disallowance rule applies where there is a qualified stock purchase by a corporation of another corporation, the acquiring corporation does not elect to treat the stock acquisition as an asset acquisition, and the acquired corporation is liquidated pursuant to a plan that is adopted within two years after the acquisition date. Further, the principal purpose for the liquidation must be the evasion or avoidance of federal income tax through the use of tax attributes that the parent would not otherwise enjoy.

The TRA provision applies to liquidations made on or after October 28, 1983, in tax years occurring after such date.

Purchase of Assets

In general, if the purchase price is greater than the book value of T's assets, then an asset acquisition may be preferable to a stock acquisition because the buyers can step up the basis of the assets for tax purposes. This generalization, of course, assumes that T does not have a net operating loss or other tax attributes that would survive in a stock transaction. The buyers will have a higher basis for depreciation purposes and for computing gain or loss on a later sale. On the other hand, as we saw earlier, if the amount paid plus liabilities is less than book value, a stock buyout is generally preferable from a tax accounting perspective, since the buyers can continue using T's higher basis.

A purchase of assets gives the buyers more flexibility in the selection of assets to purchase and liabilities to assume. Therefore, a purchase of assets allows the buyers to acquire only those assets needed for the operation of the business. By excluding unwanted assets from the buyout, the buyers can reduce both the purchase price and the financing requirements. Alternatively, a stock buyout would require the transfer of all of T's assets to the buyers, who must then dispose of any unwanted assets. Unfortunately, however, an asset purchase generally involves tax recapture to the seller and therefore impacts the selling price.

Structuring the Acquisition. In an asset acquisition, M arranges financing through A (or S). T will then transfer all of its assets to A or S in exchange for cash and/or A or S notes. T will then normally complete a plan of liquidation under Section 337 and distribute to its shareholders the consideration it receives from the sale of its assets.

Tax Treatment if T Does Liquidate under Section 337. The shareholders of T will recognize capital gain on the liquidation. The installment method of recognizing income is available to T's shareholders in those situations where T sells its assets to A for A's installment obligations, which T then distributes to its shareholders in a Section 337 liquidation. T generally will not recognize gain except for the various types of recapture items mentioned earlier.

A will get a tax basis in the acquired assets equal to the cash paid plus liabilities assumed. A cannot use T's net operating losses or other tax attributes.

Tax Treatment if T Does Not Liquidate under Section 337.   T can use the installment method of reporting income to the extent it receives notes of A. T will, however, recognize the various recapture items as ordinary income. The remaining gain is generally capital gain.

There are situations where it will be advantageous for T not to liquidate. To illustrate one such situation, let's assume that the shareholders of T are elderly and have a low tax basis for their stock. It may then be desirable to keep T alive as a Subchapter S corporation, personal holding company, or regulated investment company so the shareholders of T can benefit from a stepped-up basis for their stock at death.

Allocation of Purchase Price among Assets.   The allocation of the purchase price among the assets is a critical consideration to both parties. The buyers will be interested in negotiating the highest possible allocation to ordinary income items such as inventory, receivables, and depreciable assets and to property on which they may claim an investment credit. The seller will, quite expectedly, want the lowest possible allocation to these items, since any gain will normally be taxed as ordinary income because of depreciation recapture or because of the ordinary character of the asset.

The general rule is that allocation is made according to fair market value. However, if the buyer and seller agree on an allocation of the purchase price after arm's length bargaining by parties in adverse tax situations, the allocation agreed upon will generally be accepted by the Internal Revenue Service.

The process of negotiating the allocation of the purchase price among the assets and including the allocation in the purchase contract is often an expensive and time-consuming process. Frequently it is impossible to obtain an express allocation in the contract. For example, the sale price may be based on capitalized earnings, without regard to underlying asset values. Generally, absent an allocation agreement in the purchase contract, the purchase price will be allocated first to cash and cash equivalents, with the remainder allocated among the other assets in accordance with their relative fair market values.

ESOP Leveraged Buyouts

To extract key points from a previous chapter, an ESOP is a tax-exempt employee benefit plan that holds employer securities. There are various types of ESOPs, but only a leveraged ESOP can effectuate a leveraged buyout. A leveraged ESOP is a tax-qualified stock bonus plan or a tax-qualified stock bonus plan paired with a tax-qualified money purchase plan. An ESOP invests primarily in *"qualifying secu-*

rities" of the employer. Qualifying securities are generally defined as common stock issued by the employer which is readily tradable on an established securities market. If readily tradable common stock does not exist, then common stock of the employer will be considered qualifying if it meets certain requirements regarding voting power and dividend rights. Convertible preferred stock is also considered a qualifying security.

A leveraged ESOP can borrow funds from a third party for the purchase of employer securities, with the loan guaranteed by the employer. The ability to borrow and engage in a debt transaction with the employer corporation is a key ingredient of a successful leveraged buyout using an ESOP. For the specific structure of an ESOP LBO, please see Chapter 8.

Tax Consequences of Using an ESOP. The shareholders selling their stock to an ESOP will receive capital gain or loss treatment, since the transaction would be a sale for tax purposes. The employer corporation can deduct contributions to the ESOP up to 25 percent of the compensation paid to the employees participating in the ESOP, provided the contributions are used to pay back principal on loans used to buy employer stock. Contributions in excess of the 25 percent limit can be carried forward to future years in which the 25 percent limit is not fully used.

The Tax Reform Act of 1984 further extended the preferential treatment given leveraged ESOPs, effective for tax years beginning after July 18, 1984. First, gain on the sale of certain employer stocks to an ESOP can be deferred to the extent that the proceeds are reinvested in the stock of a domestic corporation not more than 25 percent of whose income is passive investment income. The seller must have held the stock for more than one year and must not have received the stock as compensation for services, from the exercise of a qualified stock option, or as a distribution from a qualified plan. This nonrecognition provision applies only if the ESOP still owns at least 30 percent of the total value of the employer stock outstanding after the sale, and if none of the stock purchased is allocated to the seller, the seller's family, or a person owning more than 25 percent of the employer's stock. Second, certain commercial lenders who loan funds to an ESOP for the purchase of employer stock can exclude up to 50 percent of the interest they earn on the loan. This provision is intended to encourage loans to ESOPs at reduced interest rates. Third, a corporation can take a deduction for the amount of any cash dividends paid on stock held by an ESOP.

Since the ESOP is a qualified plan, contributions and income credited to the employee-participants are not taxed until actually distributed to them, usually at retirement. These distributions are then normally taxed as ordinary income. However, a special 10-year averaging method is available if the employee receives a lump-sum distribution and has participated in the ESOP for at least five years. If income averaging is available, the ordinarily income part of the lump sum is taxed as if it were received in equal parts over 10 years. This method of determining tax liability allows part of an unusually large income to be taxed in lower brackets, so that a reduced overall tax is due.

Repayment of Loan with Pretax Dollars. A key advantage of using an ESOP to finance an LBO is that it allows the sponsoring corporation to pay off the loan to the ESOP with pretax dollars. As a result, the target's stock is paid for with tax-deductible dollars.

Tax Aspects in Financing

Retaining a Qualified Management Team. The success of a leveraged buyout often depends to a great extent on retaining the current management team. As indicated in prior chapters, outside lenders and investors do not generally like to participate in a leveraged buyout if they have to bring in a new management team to operate the target corporation. As a result of the concern over retaining the present management team, the key employees of the target corporation can normally purchase their common stock interest for a relatively modest investment. The common stock purchased by the key employees is, however, often subject to a vesting schedule based on continued employment and/or achieving certain earnings goals in the target corporation.

Four alternatives for rewarding key employees that will be discussed here are incentive stock options, restricted stock options, nonstatutory stock options, and stock appreciation rights. From a tax standpoint, all of these techniques are nonqualified plans that involve a trade-off between the corporation and the key employee as to the timing of tax and the character of income. In contrast to the tax treatment under qualified retirement and profit-sharing plans that are subject to ERISA rules, the tax consequences to the corporation and the employee resulting from these techniques occur at the same time. A basic principle is that the corporation cannot claim a tax deduction under the alternatives until such time (if ever) as the employee is taxed on income at ordinary rather than capital gain rates. As a result there generally is a built-in conflict between the tax objectives of the corporation and of its key employees, both as to timing and amount. From a tax standpoint, the corporation might be expected to prefer alternatives that permit it to claim a tax deduction as soon and in as

large an amount as possible. The employee, on the other hand, can be
expected to favor alternatives that defer the imposition of tax to a later
year and that result in capital gain rather than ordinary income.

Incentive Stock Options. A corporation may grant an employee an
Incentive Stock Option (ISO) to purchase the corporation's stock at fair
market value at the date of grant, with no tax consequence to either
the employee or the corporation at the time of issuance or exercise. For
more-than-10 percent shareholders, the option price must be 110 percent of the fair market value at the date of grant.

To qualify for this favorable tax treatment, the option must meet
several requirements. One of the requirements that deserves note sets
the annual aggregate fair market value of the underlying stock for
which any employee may be granted options, at $100,000 plus the
unused carryover from prior years. The annual carryover is half of the
difference between $100,000 and the fair market value of the stock for
which an employee was granted an option. The unused limit may be
carried over for three years.

The employee will not recognize any compensation income, and the
corporation will not receive a deduction upon the transfer or exercise of
the option. At the time of disposition, assuming that it is not disqualifying (as discussed below), the employee will recognize capital gain or
loss as measured by the difference between the proceeds received and
the employee's basis in the stock, i.e., the exercise price. Since the
employee recognizes no compensation income, the corporation will not
receive a deduction.

A disqualifying disposition will occur if the employee either disposes
of the stock prior to the requisite holding period or does not remain
continuously employed by the granting corporation or a related corporation. To retain qualification, the employee may not dispose of the
corporate stock within two years from the date the option is granted or
within one year from the date of receiving the stock upon exercise.
Further, the employee must remain continuously employed from the
period beginning on the date of the grant until three months prior to
exercise (or one year if permanently disabled).

Restricted Stock Options. A restricted stock plan, as the name
implies, involves the issuance of stock which is subject to certain restrictions. Such stock may be sold to an executive at any price the
company chooses.

Restricted stock awarded for services performed by the executive is
taxable to the recipient in the year that the property becomes freely
transferable or is no longer subject to a substantial risk of forfeiture. A
substantial risk of forfeiture exists if the executive's rights in the stock

are conditioned on the future performance of substantial services. Thus, in order to obtain the deferral of income, the executive will have to be willing to risk losing the stock if he or she leaves the company.

The amount that is taxable to the executive is the excess of the fair market value of the stock when these substantial restrictions have lapsed over the price of the stock paid by the executive. The regulations provide that fair market value is to be computed without regard to restrictions, except those restrictions which by their terms will never lapse. For example, if the stock can be sold only at a formula price set by the company and this restriction by its term will never lapse, then this formula price will be presumed to be the fair market value.

Under certain circumstances an executive, even though not currently taxed on the receipt of restricted stock, may elect to include the bargain element as personal service income under Section 83(b). This allows the executive to report any future appreciation as capital at the time of sale. The election must be made no later than 30 days after the property is transferred and cannot be revoked without the commissioner's consent. The election is made by filing two copies of a written statement with the IRS service center where the taxpayer files his return—one at the time of the election and one with the tax return for the tax year in which the property was transferred.

The Tax Reform Act of 1984 adopted a special election rule to counteract the tax court's decision in *L. Alves*, 79 TC 864. In *Alves*, the tax court ruled that the taxpayer-employee was subject to the Section 83(b) restricted property rules even though he had purchased his company's stock at its fair market value. The taxpayer had failed to elect under Section 83(b) at the time of the stock purchase to report the difference between the stock's fair market value and its cost—which difference, in this instance, would have been zero. As a result, the taxpayer was taxable at ordinary income rates on the appreciated value when his restrictions lapsed.

Under the special election rule, a taxpayer is permitted to make the election with the tax return for the first taxable year after July 18, 1984. However, the election is limited to only transfers of property in connection with the performance of services after June 30, 1976, and on or before November 18, 1982 (the date of the *Alves* decision).

The key employee who performed the services must give a copy of the written statement to the corporation for whom the services were performed. If this election is made and the executive later forfeits the property, no loss deduction is allowed despite the previous taxes paid. Thus this election should be made only after careful consideration of the potentially adverse future tax consequences.

The company will receive a tax deduction in the amount and in the year that the employee recognizes income. However, it must restore the deduction if it results from an employee's Section 83(b) election and the executive later forfeits the stock.

To illustrate this concept, let's assume that A is formed with M purchasing 10 percent of its common stock for $10 and VC purchasing 90 percent of A's common stock for $1 million. M's stock is subject to a substantial risk of forfeiture in that M must forfeit their stock to A if they cease to be full-time employees within two years and/or A fails to meet certain earnings goals.

If each member of M does not make a Section 83(b) election, they will recognize ordinary income equal to the value of A stock at the time the substantial risk of forfeiture lapses, less the $10 they paid for each share of stock. In this example, the substantial risk of forfeiture will lapse when M has been employed for two years on a full-time basis.

If each member of M makes a Section 83(b) election, the fair market value of the stock will be taxed to them when they receive it, and any later gain or loss will be capital gain in nature. Therefore, each member of M can greatly reduce the amount of ordinary income recognized by making a timely Section 83(b) election.

Nonstatutory Stock Options. Instead of receiving an immediate stock interest, a key employee can be granted a nonstatutory option to purchase shares. The option price could be whatever figure was agreed to by the parties, which can be above or below the estimated fair market value of the shares at the date of the grant.

The grant of a nonstatutory option is not a taxable event to the employee. Rather, taxable income will be realized at the time that the option is exercised, with the amount of income being the difference between the option price and the fair market value of the shares at that time. In addition, the corporation receives a deduction for the spread in the year exercised. This arrangement has several advantages, including the following:

1. As noted above, the employee is not subject to tax at the time of grant of the option.
2. The employee has considerable flexibility in terms of waiting for the shares to increase in value and in timing his exercise of the option thereafter.

A nonstatutory stock option can also have several disadvantages, including the following:

1. The amount of income subject to tax is determined by the value of the shares at the time that the option is exercised. If the value

of the shares has gone up substantially, an employee could have a significant amount of tax to pay.

2. Unless some special arrangement was made, the employee may have difficulty raising the cash with which to pay the option price and the tax that would be incurred at the time of exercise.

3. The income received by the employee will be ordinary income (subject to tax at rates of up to 50 percent) and not capital gain.

Stock Appreciation Rights. A Stock Appreciation Right (SAR) is a contract right, granted for a certain period of time, stating that an employee may receive in cash the difference between the base value of the employer's stock and the stock's value on any date during some future period. The SAR is not taxed until it is exercised. For example, if a key employee is given 1000 rights at a time when the stock is worth $25 a share and the shares go up from $25 each to $35 within the specified exercise period, he can exercise his rights at that time and receive $10,000 from his employer.

Conclusion. Just as corporations and their objectives differ, the optimal mix of executive compensation techniques will depend upon the particular circumstances. The alternatives discussed above illustrate four possibilities. If selected with understanding in the particular situation, a program can be developed that is likely to benefit both the corporation and the key employee by encouraging and rewarding superior performance.

Debt versus Equity—Section 385. The determination of whether an interest in a corporation is debt or equity has significant tax consequences. A corporate issuer of debt can deduct interest payments, and repayment of the loan is tax free to the holder of the debt. If the "interest" is really a preferred stock dividend, any payments of interest are nondeductible by the corporation, and payments of both interest and principal will be taxable as dividends to the recipient.

Section 385 authorizes the Internal Revenue Service to establish guidelines for determining whether corporate interests should be treated as debt or equity for federal tax purposes. In 1980, the first of three drafts of the Section 385 regulations regarding debt versus equity was released. The regulations were extremely complex and heavily contested, and the effective date was postponed several times. Finally, in November 1983, the regulations were withdrawn by the Internal Revenue Service. The chances of this project resurfacing appear slim.

With the withdrawal of the Section 385 regulations, there should be a return to the general guidelines of existing case law and Internal

Revenue Service rulings in determining whether the purported debt is debt or equity. Some of these factors are:

1. The debt:equity ratio—is it excessive?
2. Rights of the debtor upon default.
3. Convertibility.
4. Subordination to other creditors.
5. Maturity date.

Limitation on Interest Deduction. Section 279 may disallow the deduction otherwise allowable for interest paid or incurred on debt used in connection with the acquisition by one corporation of the stock or assets of another corporation. Section 279 defines the term *corporate acquisition indebtedness* and provides for the disallowance of interest thereon to the extent it exceeds $5 million per year. With certain exceptions, corporate acquisition indebtedness is defined as indebtedness that is:

1. Issued after October 9, 1969.
2. For the purpose of acquiring the stock or assets of another corporation.
3. Convertible into stock of the issuing corporation.
4. Subordinated to the issuing corporation's indebtedness.
5. Issued by a corporation with a debt:equity ratio greater than 2:1 or a projected earnings:annual interest ratio of 3:1 or lower.

Once an obligation has been determined to be subject to Section 279, its status cannot be altered unless (1) for any three consecutive years, the issuing corporation's debt:equity and projected earnings:annual interest ratios are proper or (2) if, in the year in which control is acquired, the debt:equity and projected earnings:annual interest ratios of the acquired and issuing corporations computed together are proper.

Section 279 can be avoided by selling the investors a current stock interest in the acquiring corporation. This is because Section 279 does not apply to an investment unit consisting of subordinated debt and common stock.

Net Operating Loss Carryover Provisions

Net operating losses incurred by a taxpayer in a particular year can generally be carried back to the three prior years to offset taxable income realized in those years. If any excess loss remains, the balance can be carried forward for 15 taxable years to offset future operating profits. Several sections of the Internal Revenue Code impose limitations on the ability of a taxpayer to utilize loss carryovers. The 1976 Tax Reform Act changed the rules on net operating loss carryovers in the case of acquisitions of loss corporations. The Tax Reform Act of 1984 generally postpones until January 1, 1986, the application of the amendments made by the Tax Reform Act of 1976. The discussion below briefly deals with the rules as they are currently in effect, without regard to the changes outlined in the 1976 Tax Reform Act or pending legislation.

Taxable Acquisitions. The net operating loss of the target corporation will not carry over to the acquiring corporation where the target's assets are acquired in a taxable transaction. Generally, the target's net operating loss will be available to the target when the shareholders of target sell their stock to the acquiring corporation. However, the net operating loss will not be available if a Section 338 election is made or if there is a change in the business of the target corporation along with a change in control. In addition, if the acquisition is motivated by the principal purpose of evading or avoiding income tax by securing the benefit of the target corporation's net operating loss, the loss carryover will be eliminated.

The consolidated return regulations provide a special rule where the target corporation joins in the filing of a consolidated return with the acquiring corporation. This rule provides that the target corporation's preacquisition net operating losses will be usable only against the target's profits and not against the profits of any other member of the consolidated group.

Participants in LBOs should always consult their tax advisers concerning the utilization of net operating loss carryovers. The rules are extremely complex and contain many traps for the unwary.

Miscellaneous Considerations. The above analysis has highlighted the major tax considerations involved in a leveraged buyout transaction. However, other tax areas should be addressed which are beyond the scope of this chapter. For example, the deductibility of start-up and organizational costs should be analyzed. State taxes must be studied, as well as the ability of the successor corporation to continue with certain payroll reporting practices of the predecessor corporation.

ACCOUNTING CONSIDERATIONS

Every LBO transaction has two financial aspects that must be considered. The first, how the transaction should be treated for tax purposes, has already been discussed. The other aspect, how the LBO is to be treated for financial reporting purposes, will now be discussed.

The two basic methods of accounting for business combinations (including LBOs) are commonly referred to as the "pooling-of-interests" and "purchase" methods. While both methods may apply to either asset or stock combinations, their application may produce dramatically different results from the standpoint of financial position and reporting of results of operations.

Accounting Principles Board Opinions (APB) Nos. 16 and 17, along with numerous interpretations and updates thereof, specify the accounting treatment to be accorded to business combinations and provide specific guidelines as to the appropriateness of the use of the two methods. A transaction that meets the criteria for a pooling must be so accounted for; otherwise the transaction must be accounted for as a purchase. A key requirement for a pooling is the use of voting common stock as the medium of exchange. This requirement restricts the type of financing usable if pooling accounting is desired.

Pooling-of-Interests Accounting

Under pooling accounting, the assets and liabilities of the seller and buyer are carried forward to the new combined entity, using the respective recorded historical cost amounts; and the reported income of the two companies is combined for both current and prior years as income of the new combined company. No revaluation of the assets of the companies is permitted.

APB No. 16 lists numerous criteria, all of which must be met in order to use pooling accounting. These criteria relate to the attributes of the combining companies, the mechanics of the exchange, and conditions arising after the exchange. These criteria are quite complex and often subject to vastly different interpretations. However, since the structure of LBOs generally contemplates the borrowing of funds to be used as payment to the target company's shareholders, the stringent requirements for the use of the pooling-of-interests method would not be met.

Purchase Accounting

If a transaction does not meet the criteria for pooling accounting, the purchase method must be used. Purchase accounting treats a business combination as a purchase of one company by another.

Determining the Cost of an Acquired Enterprise. A key factor to the purchase method is determining the cost of assets acquired in a purchase. The same accounting principles apply in determining the cost of assets acquired in a business combination as apply to acquiring assets individually. A cash payment measures the cost of assets acquired less liabilities assumed. When debt is assumed, the present value of the assumed debt usually represents its fair value. Similarly, when assets are acquired by the issuance of debt securities, the present value of amounts to be paid is the measure of cost.

A business combination may provide for the issuance of shares, transfer of cash, or other consideration contingent on specified transactions or events in the future. Often agreements provide that a portion of the consideration be placed in escrow to be distributed or returned to the transferor when specified events occur. In general, to the extent that the contingent consideration can be determined at the time of the acquisition, such amount shall be included in determining the cost of the acquired company and recorded at that time.

However, as is often the case, the amount of the contingent consideration will not be known at the time of the acquisition. As an example, additional consideration may be contingent on maintaining or achieving specified earnings levels in future periods. In these situations, when the contingency is resolved, or resolution is probable, and additional consideration is distributable, the acquiring company shall record the current fair value of the consideration issued as an additional cost of the acquired company. This subsequent recognition of additional cost will require an adjustment to the initial amounts recorded at the date of acquisition. Generally, the amount of goodwill (discussed below) will be adjusted for the amount of additional consideration issued or to be issued.

Recording Assets Acquired and Liabilities Assumed. The previous discussion considered the total cost of the assets acquired and liabilities assumed. It is also necessary to allocate this total cost to the various assets acquired and liabilities assumed.

Before dealing with some specific issues in valuing assets and liabilities, it is important to understand the general concept in allocating costs. All identifiable assets acquired (either individually or by type) and liabilities assumed (whether or not shown in the financial statement of the acquired company) shall be assigned a portion of the purchase cost of the acquired enterprise. Normally, such amounts would be equal to their fair value at the time of the acquisition, and independent appraisals may have to be used in determining the fair values of certain assets and liabilities. Subsequent sale of assets may also provide evidence of values to assign.

It is unlikely that, after all the values are assigned, the sum of the fair value of assets acquired less liabilities assumed will exactly equal the cost of the acquisition (i.e., the consideration paid). If the cost of the acquired company exceeds the sum of the fair value of identifiable assets acquired less liabilities assumed, the excess shall be recorded as goodwill. On the other hand, the sum of the values assigned to the assets less liabilities assumed may exceed the acquisition cost. In this situation, the values otherwise assignable to noncurrent assets acquired (i.e., property and equipment, intangible and other assets) are to be reduced by a proportionate part of the excess in order to determine their assigned values. Such noncurrent assets, however, may not be valued below zero. If a situation arises where all noncurrent assets have been reduced to zero and a portion of the excess still remains, a deferred credit for an excess of assigned value of identifiable assets over cost (often referred to as "negative goodwill") shall be recorded. The accounting for goodwill and negative goodwill will be covered in a later portion of this chapter.

Certain types of assets acquired and liabilities assumed usually present some unique problems in determining their fair value. The following is a summary of certain of the more common problems:

1. Inventory Valuation. Finished goods are to be valued at estimated selling prices less the sum of (*a*) costs of disposal and (*b*) a reasonable profit allowance for the selling effort of the acquiring company. The term *reasonable profit allowance for the selling effort* is intended to permit the acquiring company to report only the profits normally associated with its activities following the combination as related to the inventory items. Although the allocation of normal profit between the manufacturing effort and the selling effort will often be difficult to determine, the acquiring company is not permitted to purchase the profits already earned in the production of inventories by valuing the inventories at the acquired company's cost, and subsequently reporting the purchased profits in its income statement. Similarly, if work in process is purchased, the same criteria should apply with an additional deduction for a reasonable profit on the completion of the manufacturing process.

2. Debt Assumed. Debt of an acquired company which has a face or nominal rate of interest significantly different from a "market" rate of interest at the time of the acquisition should not be recorded at its face amount, but should be valued (based on discounting concepts) to its present value so that the true cost of the acquired company and future interest costs can be properly measured. Thus, if a company with low-interest debt is acquired at a time when interest rates have risen, the present value of the debt would be lower than the face amount.

3. Pension Liability. It may be that a company acquired in a business combination has an excess of actuarially computed value of vested benefits over the amount of its assets in the pension fund. Purchase accounting requires that a liability for pension costs should be recorded which is the greater of (a) accrued pension costs computed in conformity with the accounting policies of the acquiring corporation, or (b) the excess, if any, of the actuarially computed value of vested benefits over the amount of the pension fund assets.

4. Net Operating Loss Carryforwards. Accounting principles generally preclude the recognition of net operating loss carryforwards unless their realization can be assured beyond a reasonable doubt. Similarly, if an acquired company has net operating loss carryforwards, they should be recognized as an asset at the time of acquisition by the acquiring company only if its realization can be assured beyond a reasonable doubt. Therefore such carryforwards generally are not recorded at the time of acquisition; however, if such carryforwards are subsequently realized, the amount of the purchase price should be adjusted retroactively. The effect of this downward adjustment of the purchase price (which usually reduces goodwill) is not to allow such tax reductions to increase postacquisition income.

5. Preacquisition Contingencies of Purchased Enterprises. Unresolved contingencies may exist at the date of the acquisition which can relate to either assets or liabilities of the acquired company. If the fair value of the preacquisition contingency can be determined during the "allocation period" (which generally should not exceed one year from the consummation of a business combination) or if information available prior to the end of the allocation period indicates that it is probable that an asset existed, a liability had been incurred, or an asset had been impaired and such amount can be reasonably estimated, the amount of that preacquisition contingency should be included in the allocation of the purchase price based on its fair value. An adjustment that results from the resolution of a preacquisition contingency after the allocation period should be included in the determination of net income in the period in which the adjustment occurs.

Accounting for Tax Considerations in a Purchase. The tax effects of a business combination treated as a purchase should not be recognized in separate deferred tax accounts since a purchase assumes a new fair value allocation of the acquisition cost and any previously recorded deferred taxes are not carried over. The tax effects should, however, be considered in determining the fair values of the assets and liabilities acquired in the purchase. Thus the tax effects related to differences between otherwise current values of assets and liabilities and their tax bases should be an integral part of the determination of asset and liability carrying amounts. As such, these tax effects should be incorporated by directly adjusting the respective carrying values of the respective assets and liabilities.

In many cases the fair values of the assets exceed their tax bases, and recognition of the lack of tax basis effectively reduces the valuation base of the asset from what otherwise was its fair value. In some cases, however, certain assets acquired—for example, excess or obsolete inventories—have estimated fair values that are less than their tax bases. Recognition of these tax effects effectively increases the valuation base above its estimated fair value.

Another tax consideration which needs to be addressed when accounting for a purchase is unused investment tax credits of the acquired company. At the time of the acquisition, unused investment tax credits should not be recorded as assets. If the unused investment tax credits are realized subsequent to the acquisition, the tax benefit should be used to reduce goodwill in the period that such benefits are realized. No retroactive adjustment should be recorded to reflect the subsequent realization of unused investment tax credits, and the results of operation for previous periods should not be retroactively restated for the revised amortization of goodwill. If there is no remaining goodwill from the combination, the tax benefits should be applied to reduce any remaining amounts of noncurrent assets acquired.

Goodwill. The recorded cost of goodwill acquired after October 31, 1970, should be amortized, generally using the straight-line method, as a charge against income over the periods estimated to be benefited and should not be written off in the acquisition period. In estimating the benefited periods, the acquiring company should consider varying factors such as:

1. Legal, regulatory, or contractual provisions affecting maximum useful life.
2. Economic factors including demand for product or service, competition, and obsolescence.
3. Service lives of individuals or employees.

These, as well as other factors, may affect the determination of a reasonable useful life to be used for the amortization period. However, the period finally determined may not exceed a maximum of 40 years. Further, the period should be reevaluated continually and should be adjusted when later events or circumstances so indicate. If the acquired business is subsequently sold or liquidated, the remaining goodwill is to be considered as part of the cost of the assets (business) sold.

Negative goodwill recorded as a result of a business combination would also be amortized as a credit to income over its estimated period of benefit (not in excess of 40 years).

Pro Forma Data and Other Disclosure Requirements in the Financial Statements

Prior to 1983, all companies involved in purchases were required to disclose in the notes to their financial statements pro forma results of operations for the most current period (the period in which the acquisition occurred) to be as though the acquisition had occurred at the beginning of the period. In addition, if comparative financial statements were being presented, results of operations for the immediately preceding period were to be presented as though the companies had combined at the beginning of that period. At a minimum, disclosures were to include the effect on revenues, income before extraordinary items, net income, and earnings per share. Beginning in 1984, such disclosures were no longer required for nonpublic enterprises.

Certain other disclosures are required for all companies, whether public or nonpublic. These include the name and brief description of the acquired company, the method of accounting for the combination, the period for which the results of operations of the acquired company are included in the income statement of the acquiring company, cost of the acquisition, period and method of amortizing goodwill and any contingent payments, and options or commitments specified in the acquisition agreement and their proposed accounting treatment.

Example of Application of Purchase Accounting

The following example illustrates certain of the concepts previously discussed. The facts for the example are as follows:

Purchase Corporation (P) proposes to purchase the Seller Corporation (S), an unrelated corporation, for cash. P requests an analysis of the financial reporting and effects of the acquisition. The following is S's balance sheet at September 30, 1984, together with supplemental notes. Appraised values for balance sheet items in the aggregate exceed book values. The shareholders of S will sell their stock for $10 million cash.

S CORPORATION
Balance Sheet
September 30, 1984
(in thousands of dollars)

	Historical carrying basis	Selected or determined appraised values
Assets		
Current assets:		
Cash	$ 100	
Trade accounts receivable (net of reserve for doubtful accounts $50) (Note 1) . . .	900	$ 850
Inventories (Note 2)	800	1,500
Prepaid expenses, deposits, etc.	100	100
Total current assets	$1,900	
Plant and equipment (Note 3):		
Land	100	$ 500
Plant 1	2,000	4,000
Plant 2	1,000 3,100	1,000 5,500
Investment in unconsolidated subsidiary (Note 4)	300	500
Goodwill (Note 5)	200	1,000
Total assets	$5,500	
Liabilities and Stockholders' Equity		
Current liabilities:		
Accounts payable	$ 200	
Current portion of long-term debt	400	
Accrued federal and state income taxes (Note 6)	500	
Accrued expenses	100	
Total current liabilities	$1,200	
Long-term debt (Note 3)	2,000	
Deferred federal and state income taxes (Note 6)	500	
Commitments and contingencies (Notes 7 and 8)	—	
Total liabilities	3,700	
Stockholders' equity	1,800	
Total liabilities and stockholders' equity . . .	$5,500	
Stockholders' equity is represented by:		
Capital stock	$1,000	
Paid-in capital	400	
Accumulated earnings	400	
	$1,800	

Notes to financial statements

Note 1: Accounts Receivable

- The realizable value of accounts receivable is determined to be $850, therefore the reserve for doubtful accounts should be increased by $50.

Note 2: Inventories

	Replacement cost	FIFO cost	Costs of completion
Raw materials	$200	$100	$600
Work in process	—	300	200
Finished goods	—	400	—
	$200	$800	$800

	Selling price of finished products	Profit allowance for		
		Completion	Selling effort	Cost of disposal
Raw materials	$1,500	$600	$ 90	$ 90
Work in process	1,000	200	50	50
Finished goods	840	—	20	20
	$3,340	$800	$160	$160

- *Supplies inventory*—Cost of supplies are written off as incurred. At September 30, 1984, supplies on hand had a replacement cost of $100 and a cost of $75.

Note 3: Plant and Equipment
- The land account reflects the cost of vacant land not required in Seller's businesses.
- The appraised value of the operating assets are based on an existing market for the assets.
- Costs, accumulated depreciation, and replacement cost are as follows:

	Accounting and tax basis	Replacement cost
Land	$ 100	$ 500
Plant 1:		
Cost	$2,500	
Accumulated book depreciation	500	
Net book value	2,000	
Excess of tax over book depreciation	750	
Tax basis	$1,250	$4,500
Plant 2:		
Cost	$3,000	
Accumulated book depreciation	2,000	
Net book value	1,000	
Excess of tax over book depreciation	250	
Tax basis	$ 750	$1,000

- All depreciation was accumulated after 1969 and is subject to recapture.
- Long-term debt of $2,400 consists of a mortgage on Plant 1 which bears interest at 8 percent a year and is payable ratably over the next six years.

Note 4: Investment in Unconsolidated Subsidiary
- Seller owns 50 percent of the outstanding stock of ABC Inc., a nonpublic corporation which conducts a business unrelated to that of Seller. This investment is accounted for under the equity method for financial statement purposes, as follows:

	Accounting basis	Equity in replacement costs of underlying assets, less liabilities
Cost	$100	
Share of increase in equity	200	
	$300	$400

Note 5: Goodwill
- Goodwill of $200 arose from the taxable acquisition of XYZ several years ago. Subsequently, XYZ was merged into Seller and is now an operating division of Seller.
- Seller developed a patent which it uses in its business. Costs of $125 for developing this patent, which has 10 years to run, were expensed in prior years for both accounting and tax purposes. The patent has a replacement cost of $450 and an appraised value of $500.

Note 6: Federal and State Income Taxes
- Accrued federal and state income taxes of $500 represent estimated taxes for the current year.
- Deferred federal income taxes are the result of the difference between book and tax depreciation.

	Excess of tax depreciation	Deferred tax
Plant 1	$ 750	$375
Plant 2	250	125
	$1,000	$500

Note 7: Long-term Leases
- Seller rents several office locations in various parts of the country. Leases were entered into for rents lower than current rates. The present value of rental savings is $100.

Note 8: Pension
- No accrued pension costs are required on Seller's balance sheet under its present accounting policies. A change to Purchaser's pension cost accounting policies is likely after the acquisition. Accrued pension costs computed in conformity with the accounting policies of Purchaser for its pension plan are $100.
- A portion of Seller's pension plan note to financial statements is as follows:

Actuarial present value of accumulated plan benefits	
Vested	$ 600
Nonvested	800
	$1,400
Net assets available for plan benefits	$ 400

Solution to the Example

S CORPORATION
Balance Sheet
September 30, 1984
(in thousands of dollars)

	Historical carrying basis	Purchase adjustments add (subtract)	As adjusted
Assets			
Cash	$ 100	—	$ 100
Receivables (Note A)	900	$ (25)	875
Inventories (Note B)	800	350	1,150
Supplies (Note C)	—	50	50
Prepaid expenses, deposits, etc.	100	—	100
Land (Note D)	100	280	380
Plant 1 (Note E)	2,000	625	2,625
Plant 2 (Note F)	1,000	(125)	875
Investment in affiliate (Note G)	300	80	380
Goodwill (Note K)	200	6,075	6,275
Patents (Note H)	—	250	250
Long-term leases (Note H)	—	50	50
Total assets	$5,500	$7,610	$13,110
Liabilities and Stockholders' Equity			
Accounts payable	$ 200	—	$ 200
Accruals:			
Income taxes	500	—	500
Other	100	—	100
Long-term debt (Note J)	2,400	$ (190)	2,210
Customer deposits	—	—	—
Deferred taxes	500	(500)	—
Unfunded pension costs (Note I)	—	100	100
Total liabilities	3,700	590	3,110
Stockholders' equity	1,800	8,200	10,000
Total liabilities and stockholders' equity	$5,500	$7,610	$13,110

Notes to Computation of Cost Allocation

Note A: Receivables

Accounts receivable	$950
Reserve for bad debts	100
Fair value	850
Tax basis	900
Difference	50
Tax effect of difference at 50 percent tax rate	25
Record ($850 + $25)	875
Adjustment ($875 − $900)	($ 25)

Note B: Inventories—FIFO
  • Summary:

	Historical carrying basis	Fair value
Raw materials	$100	$ 200
Work in process	300	500
Finished goods	400	800
	$800	$1,500

  • Fair value computed as follows:

Raw materials		
At replacement cost (used only for raw materials)		$ 200
Work in process		
Selling price		$1,000
Less:		
Cost of completion	$200	
Cost of disposal	50	
Profit allowance for:		
Completion	200	
Selling effort	50	500
Fair value		$ 500
Finished goods		$ 840
Selling price		
Less:		
Cost of disposal	20	
Profit allowance for selling effort (not for manufacturing effort, unlike work in process)	20	40
Fair value		$ 800
Fair value		$1,500
Tax basis		800
Difference		700
Tax effect of difference at 50 percent tax rate		350
Record ($1,500 − $350)		1,150
Adjustment ($1,150 − $800)		$ 350

Note C: Supplies

Fair value	$ 100
Tax basis	—
Difference	100
Tax effect of difference at 50 percent tax rate	50
Record ($100 − $50)	$ 50

Note D: Land

Fair value	$ 500
Tax basis	100
Difference	400
Tax effect of difference at 30 percent tax rate (effective capital gain rate)	120
Record ($500 − $120)	380
Adjustment ($380 − $100)	$ 280

Note E: Plant 1

Cost	$2,500
Accumulated depreciation	500
	2,000
Excess tax depreciation over book depreciation	750
Tax basis	1,250
Fair value	4,000
Difference	2,750
Tax effect of difference at 50 percent tax rate	1,375
Record ($4,000 − $1,375)	2,625
Adjustment ($2,625 − $2,000)	$ 625

Note F: Plant 2

Cost	$3,000
Accumulated depreciation	2,000
	1,000
Excess tax depreciation over book depreciation	250
Tax basis	750
Fair value	1,000
Difference	250
Tax effect of difference at 50 percent tax rate	125
Record ($1,000 − $125)	875
Adjustment ($875 − $1,000)	($ 125)

Note G: Investment in Affiliate

Cost	$ 100
Fair value	500
Difference	400
Tax effect of difference at 30 percent tax rate (effective capital gain rate)	120
Record ($500 − $120)	380
Adjustment ($380 − $300)	$ 80*

* Note: The $80 excess over underlying equity in affili-
ate of $300 is to be amortized in the same manner as
goodwill.

Note H: Other Assets

	Patents	Long-term leases
Fair value	$500	$100
Tax effect at 50 percent tax rate (no tax base)	250	50
Record	$250	$ 50

Note I: Unfunded Pension Costs
   • This liability is the greater of:

Accrued pension cost computed in conformity with the accounting policies of acquirer for its pension plan	$100

or

The excess of the actuarially computed value of vested benefits over the amount of the pension fund ($600 − $400)	$200
Accrued pension cost	$200
Tax effect at 50 percent tax rate	100
Record	$100

Note J: Long-Term Debt
   • Considering the current money market and the credit rating of Seller Corporation, assume a 14 percent interest rate is appropriate, and therefore the present value of the mortgage is $2,019.

Tax basis	$2,400
Present value	2,019
Difference	381
Tax effect of difference at 50 percent	191
Record ($2,019 + $191)	2,210
Adjustment ($2,210 − $2,400)	$ 190

Note K: Goodwill
   • The historical carrying amount of goodwill ($200) is not evaluated. The goodwill of $6,275 is determined by the residual method (balancing adjustment).

Conclusion

And so we have come full circle. We have linked the needs of the seller with the capacity of the buyer and pointed out the financing, tax, accounting, and legal aspects that bridge the two. The rest is up to you.

Index